Simple Strategies for Spiritual Warfare

Harold F. Hunter, Th.D.

Trinity Academic Press

Trinity Academic Press

World Wide Web: Trinitysem.edu
Email:Contact@trinitysem.edu

©1983 by Harold F. Hunter. Edited for 2015 publication by Braxton Hunter

All Scripture quotations taken from the King James Version of the Bible.

ISBN-13: 978-0692563762 (Trinity Academic Press)
ISBN-10: 0692563768

Printed in the United States of America

DEDICATION

To my wife, Marilyn, for her unswerving love and support during the years of my ministry, and for the superior example she sets as the greatest Christian I know; to my sons, Chad and Braxton, for the strength and joy their daily presence gives me.

Table of Contents

Chapter One

How to VIEW THE BIBLE

Every conflict in the human experience demands an authoritative procedure if success is to be enjoyed. No less is that true in the realm of spiritual warfare. To sally forth into combat against the prince of darkness without adequate preparation is folly. It is comforting to know that our Lord has anticipated that need and has provided his children with clear instructions for victorious living in His written Word — indeed, the Word of God.

It stands to reason, therefore, that Satan's first line of attack has been directed against the trustworthiness of the Scriptures. The battle of the ages still rages, and the battleground is the authority of God's Book. Our greatest contemporary struggle is not in the arena of human rights nor international economic policies nor in protracted debates concerning the nuclear freeze. Rather, it is whether God's own people will continue to accept, live and proclaim every line of the Bible as true and, in fact, "God-breathed." We believe it to be so for Paul declares in II Timothy 3:16-17:

All scripture is given by inspiration of God, and is profitable for doctrine, for reproof, for correction, for instruction in righteousness, that the man of God may be perfect, thoroughly furnished unto all good works.

The word, "inspiration," as found in this verse, is the Greek word, "theopneustos," which means, "God- breathed." We certainly do not believe that God has bad breath for verse 16 begins by saying, "All scripture is given by inspiration of God . . ."

Does that word, "all," include the books of the New Testament? Does the Bible ever declare that the same. authority and scriptural designation should be granted them? Turn to II Peter 3:15-16.

And account that the longsuffering of our Lord is salvation, even as our beloved brother, Paul, also according to the wisdom given unto him hath written unto you; as also in all his epistles, speaking in them of these things, in which are some things hard to be understood, which they that are unlearned and unstable wrest, as they do also the other scriptures, unto their own destruction.

Did you note the phrase, . . as they do also the other scriptures . . ."? Peter was affirming that the letters of Paul were to be regarded with the same scriptural integrity as were the writings of the Old Testament.

However, the controversy centers itself around the validity and accuracy of the Old Testament, particularly the Book of Genesis, more than any of the books of the New Testament. The creeping paralysis of secular humanism, which has so invaded every facet of modern society that to question its findings at all is to present oneself as illiterate, says Genesis is only mythological.

If Satan can somehow cast the slightest doubt on the trustworthiness of any verse in the Scriptures, he will then have sufficient foundation from which to launch his attack on the passages that concern themselves with the fundamental doctrines of the Christian faith.

Satan has been a rebel from the very beginning. He detests authority. The reason for his expulsion from the presence of God is quite easily seen in Isaiah 14:12-15. Please note the number of times Satan uses the phrase, "I will.'? Openly, and with sinful arrogance, Satan reveals his rebellious nature;

How art thou fallen from heaven, O Lucifer, son of the morning! How art thou cut down to the ground, who didst weaken the nations! For thou hast said in thine heart, I will ascend into heaven, I will exalt my throne above the stars of God; I will sit also upon the mount of the congregation, in the sides of the north, I will ascend above the heights of the clouds, I will be like the Most High. Yet, thou shalt be brought down to hell, to the-sides of the pit.

Five times Satan challenged God s authority by belligerently asserting "I will!"

God's divine plan for order by conforming to a chain of authority was snubbed by the devil. Please understand! There is a chain of command in spiritual matters, in church, in government, in education, in the home. In fact, in every segment of human society where there exists interpersonal relationships, there also exists a definite order of control. When a person rebels against authority, whether it is civil, ecclesiastical, educational or whatever, he is a fool to proudly call himself a "rugged individualist" who is "doing his own thing." He is actually following Satan!

"But," you say, "What about those times of dire oppression when a stand must be taken?" Be very careful. The only times we are permitted to reject authority is when that authority comes into direct conflict with God's will and Word for our lives. In Acts 5:29 we are granted that privilege when the Scriptures declare that ". . . we ought to obey God rather than men." That, dear friend, is the only exception to God's expectations for our conformity to His rule.

Paul takes up the authority issue in Romans 13:1-7. In the following presentation of those verses, we have printed certain phrases in bold letters when the phrases are especially relevant to the issue at hand. To appreciate the full meaning of Paul's words, you need to remember that the Christian community has never suffered more heinous persecution than it did at the hands of the Roman government. But observe the attitude toward the government that the believer was expected to exhibit.

LET EVERY SOUL BE SUBJECT UNTO THE HIGHER POWERS. For there is no power but of God; the powers that be are ordained of God. WHOSOEVER, THEREFORE, RESIST ET H THE POWER, RESIST ETH THE ORDINANCE OF GOD: AND THEY THAT RESIST SHALL RECEIVE TO THEMSELVES DAM NATION. For rulers are not a terror to good works, but to the evil. Wilt thou, then, not be afraid of the power? Do that which is good, and thou shalt have praise of the same: For HE IS THE MINISTER OF GOD to thee for good. But if thou do that which is evil, be afraid; for HE" BEARET H NOT THE SWORD IN VAIN: for HE IS THE MINISTER OF GOD, a revenger, to execute wrath upon him that doeth evil Wherefore, YE MUST NEEDS BE SUBJECT, not only for wrath but also for conscience sake. For, for this cause PAY YE TRIBUTE ALSO: for THEY ARE GOD'S MINISTERS, attending continually upon this very thing. RENDER, THEREFORE, TO ALL THEIR DUES: tribute to whom tribute is due; custom to whom custom; fear to whom fear; honor to whom honor.

Just look at how many references stand out in written testimony to God's description of pagan rulers as MINISTERS OF GOD. If God is displeased with disobedience to pagan rule, HOW MUCH MORE IS HIS DIVINE HOLINESS INCENSED BY A BLATANT DISREGARD FOR ANY PART OF HIS WRITTEN WORD? God's own view of His Word is that it is to be in the place of His own highest exaltation Liberal "theologians" have nightmares with Psalm 138 2 which firmly declares,

I will worship toward thy holy temple, and praise thy name for thy loving kindness and for thy truth FOR THOU HAS MAFNIFIED THY WORD ABOVE ALL THY NAME

Satan cannot refute the Word by labeling the Bible as a collection of lies A few spiritual morons might accept that ploy, but the masses will not Therefore, he is forced to operate by implanting doubts concerning the Scriptures' historical and scientific accuracy while being very careful to praise the Bible as good ancient literature Nowhere does he use this device more adroitly than in a modern public school system that is heavily dominated by secular humanism a philosophy that holds man as ac countable only to himself and, as a philosophy, either directly or indirectly rejects the existence of a Higher Power What cannot be described by the methodology of the scientific community is tossed aside with a scoff by an unbelieving intelligentsia To them science is always right faith is always wrong

The absurdity of that pseudo-scientific position is often repeated in the Scriptures to the much chagrin of the Bible's detractors. Take, for example, a statement by Job in the twenty-sixth chapter of the book bearing his name. The Book of Job is the oldest book in the Bible and was written at a point in human history when the known world was under the heavy domination of the Babylonians who firmly believed as reliable scientific fact that the world was on the back of an elephant, the elephant was on the back of a turtle, and the turtle was floating around in a cosmic sea of nothingness. Amid the jeers and taunts of the best-trained minds of the Babylonian school, Job took his stance that, ". . . He hangeth the earth upon nothing" (26:7). You can imagine the guffaws as those poor stupid "logically-minded" men asserted that any person with a modicum of reason would surely know that everything has to hang from something or sit on something. To those queries, Job must have replied—and this is a very important Biblical principle, that a particularly obscure and ambiguous statement does not necessarily have to meet the requirements of human logic. Given time, most of these such "impossible" statements will be corroborated by yet undiscovered proofs. In this particular case, man was finally forced, after the passage of centuries, to agree with the itinerant preacher, Job, and disagree with his erudite and well-informed debaters.

The prophet, Isaiah, ministered some seven hundred years prior to the coming of Jesus as the Incarnate Son of the Living God. Yet, in those ancient days he made an amazing statement that even he himself would have had difficulty explaining, outside of his faith in the absolute integrity of the Word of God. He says, in chapter forty and verse twenty-two of his book, that "it is he who sitteth on the circle of the earth . . ." This word, "circle," is not used to denote a flat geometric circle; rather, it conveys what may be best defined in the English language as a "globe." Therefore, the verse is better translated, "It is he who sitteth on the globe of the earth . . ." Again, as with Job, it took hundreds of years to "prove" what God's Word had already established.

"But," the skeptic responds, "Those people lived in a different age. They were primitives who were blindly groping for meaning in the dawn of man's emergence from a lower creature order. We would never be guilty of reach- ing such ridiculous and stupid conclusions as those poor dupes."

Is that so? When man finally reached the moon's surface and returned, some interesting comments were made at one of the press conferences. It was noted by our space travelers that there were canals on the moon's surface, very much like the ridges on the headlamps of our automobiles. Further, they shared that all over the surface of the moon were sprinkled glass-like particles (titanium). The brilliant scientific conclusion was that, if one did not know better, it might be deduced that the moon had actually been placed in the sky to give light by night. Of course, man's modem sophistication is just as laughable as that of his long-dead forefather. In Genesis 1:16, the Scriptures declare in simplicity,

"And God made two great lights; the greater light to rule the day, and the lesser light to rule the night."

So much for contemporary man's superior perception.

More than in any other area, however, Satan is directing the main thrust of his attack on the origin of man. The reason is quite obvious. There are many apparent contradictions in the Scriptures, such as the ones I have already presented, which yield themselves to the scrutiny of unbiased scientific investigation. Yet, because these seeming contradictions can be disproved by concrete statements, they are not very useful as artillery in Satan's arsenal. What he needs, and has in the theory of evolution, is a proposition that cannot be definitely proven or disproven.

For example, in Charles Darwin's book, The Origin of the Species, the statement of preface to many of his "scientific" findings is, "We may well suppose . . ." Over eight hundred times in his book that phrase is found. In God's Word, however, the statement is never found at all. Instead, God's faithful men thunder triumphantly, "Thus saith the Lord!"

Nevertheless, we who believe the Bible are presented as half-illiterate, anachronistic, anti-intellectual beings who have built an entire idea on the flimsiest of foundations, namely, faith. Several years ago I had an opportunity to share a witness with a very well~versed evolutionist and
was amazed at some of evolution's conclusions. Let me cite two or three.

This enlightened professor of biology said that the reason we often dream of falling but never of landing is because millions of years ago our primal ancestors —ape-like creatures — slept in the trees as a means of security against their predators. Their greatest fear was the possibility of falling to the ground below and thereby being injured, killed, or devoured by their enemies. The ones that did fall and died never had offspring after that tragic occurrence. However, those that remained in the treetops had their fears reinforced as they witnessed the sad demise of their unfortunate comrades. As a result, their offspring developed a similar dread, as did the next generation, and the next generation, and etc. So, now you know why you may dream of falling but never of landing.

I was also interested in the reasons this brilliant biological marvel gave for the development of the various parts of the human anatomy. Take, for example. the nose. Eons and eons ago, he asserted, a freckle-like protrusion erupted on the noseless face of our very primitive ancestor. The sun's rays, along with a complicated set of unique environmental conditions, caused that small protrusion to begin a process of growth. Hundreds of generations and millions of years later, the nose reached its full development. To that preposterous hypothesis I retorted, "Well, we are blessed indeed that the freckle was on our face instead of our big toe or else we would have gone around smelling sweaty socks all day." He did not find that to be humorous.

It is quite obvious that although the scientific com- munity prides itself in being "anti-faith" and thoroughly "clinical" in its development of laws and theories, it is evident that what the evolutionist believes about the origin of man requires more faith than even what the Bible says. Actually, the evolutionist believes, but cannot explain, that nothing plus nothing equals everything. And even that opinion, which is basic in the theory of evolution, is found in opposition to another of their iron- clad principles, the second law of thermodynamics, which states that everything in existence is in the process of deteriorating from the complex to the

Simple. But, in violation of that very valid rule, the evolutionist will argue that all of life, human and otherwise, developed
from the simplicity of one small cell to the complexity of the world's multi-organic systems.

'The Biblical discussion of man's origin is recorded on the opening pages of the Book of Genesis. As you perhaps already know, the first eleven chapters have been the object of the critic's derisive scorn. Especially those of liberal theology have had their fun as they have caricatured those of conservative theology as insecure adults who required a Bible without error for their own emotional stability. They maintain that it does not really matter what one believes concerning the origin of man or any of the other "myths" in the Book of Genesis. What is really important is that people become God-conscious and live according to the love-principles set forth by Jesus.

A good question for consideration, then, is very simply, "Can a person be saved and believe in evolution?" Is what a person believes about man's creation really secondary to faith in Christ, or is it part of the requisite one must possess in order to have the necessary faith to believe in Christ? Without question, the Bible, by precept and direct statement, makes it crystal clear that anyone who denies the authenticity and trustworthiness of Genesis cannot possibly he saved. That. of course, would include the evolutionist. Let's now look at three reasons why this is so.

First, there is a SYMBOLIC reason. God has a formula for the creation of light. That formula is S+W=L, which means, "Spirit plus Word equals Light." You will find the formula first employed in Genesis 1:2-3:

And the earth was without form, and void; and darkness was upon the face of the deep. And the Spirit of God moved upon the face of the waters. And God said, Let there be light: and there was light.

Please note that the "Spirit moved" (S) and "God said" (W) and the result was "light" (L).

Now, turn to II Corinthians 4:3-6 for God's next use of this same formula:

But" if our gospel be hid, it is hid to them that are lost: In whom the god of this world hath blinded the minds of them which believe not, lest the light of the glorious gospel of Christ, who is the image of God, should shine unto them. For we preach not ourselves, but Christ Jesus the Lord; and ourselves your servants for Jesus' sake. For God, who commanded the light to shine out of darkness, hath shined in our hearts, to give the light of the knowledge of the glory of God in the face of Jesus Christ.

There you have it! Paul is saying that he believes the literal interpretation of Genesis chapter one. He says that in precisely the same manner by which God caused light to enter the darkness of the physical world, He has also caused light to enter the darkness of man's spiritual world. "For God (S, because "God is a spirit") plus "commanded" (W) equals "light" (L). If a person rejects Paul's authority in this statement of belief about salvation then his authority must also be questioned in Acts 16:31 where he says, "Believe on the Lord Jesus Christ and thou shalt be saved."

You will remember that at the first of this chapter we established that II Peter 3:15-16 specifically names Paul as a man through whom the Word of the Lord was given. In fact, this phrase, ". . . as also in all his epistles. . . which they that are unlearned and unstable wrest (distort), as they do also the OTHER SCRIPTURES" (II Peter 3: 16), gives Paul equal billing with the men of God of the Old Testament period. Why is this significant? The same requirements of God for those men would also stand true for Paul. And what was that requirement? Deuteronomy 18:22 states it clearly:

And if thou say in thine heart, How shall we know the word which the Lord hath not spoken? When a prophet speaketh in the name of the Lord, if the thing follow not, nor come to pass, that is the thing which the Lord hath not spoken, but the prophet hath spoken it presumptuously: thou shalt not be afraid of him.

In other words, if Paul ever presumed himself to speak for the Lord and something he shared was actually false, then according to the above Scriptures, he was not a true man of God and nothing he said could be trusted. If a person rejects Paul's statement in II Corinthians 4:3-6 concerning the validity of the creation account as found in Genesis chapter one, he is then forced into the position of rejecting Paul's salvation message. of Acts 16:31 because of the injunction of Deuteronomy eighteen. So, because of symbolism, a man cannot believe in evolution and be saved.

Second, there is the reason of the SAVIOR. The Book of Genesis was authored by Moses. Did Jesus believe the things found written in Genesis? To answer that question we must turn to John 5:45-46:

Do not think that I will accuse you to the Father: there is one that accuseth you, even Moses, in whom ye trust. For had ye believed Moses, ye would have believed me: for he wrote of me. BUT IF YE BE- LIEVE NOT HIS WRITINGS, HOW SHALL YE BELIEVE MY WORDS.

This statement by the Lord Jesus should bring a disquieting feeling to the heart of every reader. Our Lord is actually saying that the person who cannot believe the Book of Genesis places himself in the position of being unable to believe the Book of John. Quite literally, if one cannot. believe Genesis 1, 2, 3 about the "birth" of the world, Jesus says he cannot believe John 1, 2, 3 about the "new birth" of the believer. Please note that these are the words of Jesus. By reason of what the Savior said, a man cannot believe in evolution and be saved.

Third, there is the reason of SALVATION. The evolutionist says that there was not a specific first man by the name of Adam. If that is true, then Adam never sinned. If Adam never sinned, then the sin nature was not introduced into the human family. If the sin nature was not introduced into the human family, then there was no need for a sacrifice for sins. If there was no need for a sacrifice for sins, then there was no need for the death of Jesus at Calvary. So, by reason of SALVATION a man cannot believe in evolution and be saved.

This chapter has been written to bolster flagging faith in the scriptural quest. The war is raging and God's participants are - sometimes faint, despite their innermost desire to be otherwise. No matter how arduous your task or seemingly impossible your situation, the Bible can be trusted as a foolproof and thoroughly dependable guide for personal victory and fulfillment. It is, without any doubt at all, THE WORD OF GOD.

PRACTICAL APPLICATIONS
for
"How to View the Bible"

1. By use of sources other than the Bible, develop your own definition of the following terms as they relate to the Word of God:

(1) Infallible

(2) Verbally-inspired

(3) Inerrant

(4) Literal

(5) Plenary

2. Contact the individual most responsible for your appreciation of God's Word and ask him/her to share with you why the Bible is so very important. Enter a brief summary of that person's response in the space below.

3. Ask two elderly saints to recall for you the times in their lives when the Bible was of greatest assistance. When completed, ask them to sign their names in the space below with the location of their favorite Bible verse.

4. If you can mean it, pray this prayer and sign your name:

Dear Lord, I have not studied your Word as faithfully as I should. Beginning today, I will sincerely TRY to read at least one verse each day and pray for your guidance and understanding. If I become so busy that I miss a day, I will not let Satan destroy this intention by causing guilt. I have promised you that I will try. Help me keep this commitment. I do want and need your Word. In the name of Jesus, I pray. Amen.

_____

Signed

_____

Date

Chapter Two

How to Have Assurance Of Salvation

If a poll is ever taken to determine the most frequently asked question among those of the Christian community, there is little doubt about what that question will be, namely, "How can I be sure that I have really been saved, that I have truly been born again?" The assurance of one's salvation is at the very heart of the believer's relationship with God. He cannot possibly perform the expected services, grow in grace, bear positive fruit, or confidently meet his adversary unless forever settled in his heart is the certainty of his own salvation. It seems that every Christian is destined to struggle with that question at some point in his spiritual development; the problem is apparently of universal scope throughout the length and breadth of Christendom!

Contrary to viewing the emergence of this problem in an individual's life as an evidence of his spiritual deterioration, perhaps we should really begin to see it as a possible indicator of his desire to grow. As just mentioned, the believer cannot grow until this critical issue is settled, but God can use this doubt as an irritation uncomfortable enough to drive the suffering saint toward self-judgment and a more serious study of the Word. When that happens, there are side benefits that often accrue to him. Those benefits include the finding of other scriptural nuggets which will adorn his search for truth with extra beauty. Almost without realizing it, he develops a renewed love for Jesus. Many great men and women of God have looked back from the perspective of succeeding years, after having encountered this doubt, and have rejoiced that it was the beginning point of their rapid movement toward spiritual maturity.

Satan delights in harassing and tormenting the believer by repeatedly whispering in his ear, But you cannot know . . . you cannot know . . - You Cannot know Uncertainty slowly increases to doubt, and unchecked doubt can change to fear. Fear will paralyze the best intentions of even the most highly motivated person of integrity. Can we know? In I John 5:13 are these words

These things have I written unto you that believe on the name of the Son of God; that YE MAY KNOW THAT YE HAVE ETERNAL LIFE, and that ye may believe on the name of the Son of God.

In order to nullify this lack of assurance , we need to establish one fundamental foundation onslaught upon which can be built an adequate defense against this onslaught of the devil. Basically, it must be clearly understood that although we are saved by the blood, we have confidence by the Word. At the forefront of' all scriptural truth, then, is the trustworthiness of God s World. Peace in the very midst of terrible adversity is possible only through an unswerving belief that God will do exactly what He has said that He will do. A key verse in support of the veracity of our Lord is Titus 1:2 which declares:

In hope of eternal life, which GOD, THAT CANNOT LIE, promised before the world began.

Let us now take an imaginary journey back through time until we come to the crossing of the Red Sea. God has given His people the Promise of His divine protection as they passed through the water on dry grounds

AND THE LORD SAID unto Moses, Wherefore criest thou unto me? Speak unto the children of Israel, that they go forward; but lift thou up thy rod, and stretch out thine hand over the sea, and divide it: and the CHILDREN OF ISRAEL SHALL GO ON DRY GROUND THROUGH THE MIDST OF THE SEA (Exodus 14:15-16).

As we arrive on this scene, we find heated arguments and clamorous discussions being held by small clusters of people throughout the camp of the Israelites. Many want to go; many want to stay. Certain pessimistic Jews are fearful of the two gigantic walls of water between which they have been commanded to walk. If either of those walls come crashing down, immediate death will ensue.

Even if Pharaoh is rushing from behind in hot pursuit of this fugitive band of his former slaves, there is at this present time a sense of security. Perhaps that feeling of safety is temporary at best, but unquestionably they are safe for the moment. Something must be said for that. Too, no one has ever crossed a river in the way that they are now being asked. They have no lesson from history upon which they can lean for support. There is only one thing that separates the people into those who are optimistic and those who are pessimistic, into those who want to go and those who want to stay. That one thing is the Word of God.

One of the Israelites says to Moses, "Now Moses, are you sure that you got the instructions right? Don't you think we ought to build some rafts, just in case? Even better, why don't you first send a scout across by himself while we all watch, and then we will all have a sign that God is really in it. Now, Moses, don't get me wrong! I believe God as much as anybody, but we have too much at stake to be wrong!"

As Moses turns and glances toward the growing cloud of dust on the horizon that denotes the coming of Pharaoh's army, another of the Jews approaches him. He encourages the wearied leader by saying, "Moses, if God said it, that settles it, so let's go!" With that, this happy Jew heads toward the path between the water.

When they finally arrive on the opposite shore, which of these two Jews will have been the safest? They will both have been equally safe. However, the second Jew will have had a thoroughly enjoyable time, while the first will have reluctantly marched across, thinking every step would surely be his last. What is the difference? The difference is that one believed the Word for assurance while the other did not.

SALVATION IS INITIATED BY THE HOLY SPIRIT

In establishing assurance, we must begin at the time of the believer's presumed salvation experience. What happened at that time is very important! Did the individual go forward in a meeting with a group of his childhood friends only because it was "the thing to do ? Did he make a purely emotional decision? Did he follow a false plan of salvation? Did he go forward to satisfy the expectations of a person important to him? Did he make an honest, sincere, and Biblical commitment?

When the motive is uncovered, we expose the reasons for the huge numbers of people who make professions of faith and are baptized but are never seen again after coming from the water. More than an intellectual acceptance of even the right plan is essential for salvation; the individual must be spiritually quickened and drawn by the right man. It is not the plan of salvation that saves; it is the man of salvation who saves. This pull of the Spirit is emphasized in John 6:44:

No man can come to me, EXCEPT THE FATHER WHICH HATH SENT ME DRAW HIM: and I will raise him up in the last day.

The following comments may run counter with what you have always believed, but John 6:44 urges that we take a second look. Pagans, as well as many who have lulled themselves into a Christian slumber, have built a "relationship with God" on "soul-enlightenment."

Soul enlightenment refers to man's emotions. The word for "soul" in the Greek New Testament is "psyche," from which we get "psychology" and "psychiatry." Every man's emotional self will he sufficiently illuminated at some point in his life to cause him at least a moment of reflection concerning his relationship with God. John 1:9, speaking of Jesus, shares:

That was the true light, WHICH LIGHTETH EVERY MAN THAT COMETH INTO THE WORLD.

Unfortunately, when a man experiences that soul enlightenment, he will often "join the system" with which he is most familiar. in America, where patriotism and Christianity seem almost one-and-the-same to the casual observer, he becomes a Christian. In

Saudi Arabia, he becomes a Moslem; in Israel, he becomes a Jew. His soul (emotional self) has been enlightened. He sees his need of God. He joins the system, and stays lost.

This sad occurrence is too frequently repeated in the lives of children who have been raised in Christian homes. They have learned the right answers, know the right words, and can recite the right plan. Finally, the little child is brought to the pastor's study for a determination by him of the child's spiritual maturity in making a valid decision. Has the child come to a time that he should "join the system," or does he sense a definite divine pull accompanied by an awful sense of spiritual hopelessness? Multitudes of sincere soul-enlightened children who were programmed and processed, brain-washed and baptized, and have followed all of this with a non-Christian lifestyle, cast doubt upon the validity of reading John 3:16 and praying a prayer without the quickening power of the Spirit:

And YOU HATH HE QUICKENED, who were dead in trespasses and sins (Ephesians 2:1).

This quickening of the Spirit we might aptly call "spirit enlivenment." A surge of Holy Ghost energy sparks man's innermost being, his spirit, and initiates that wondrous drawing power on the individual's heart. That pull of the Spirit is commonly termed "the conviction of the Holy Ghost." It is possible to accept Christ as Lord only when this spirit enlivenment occurs. A person cannot choose the timing of his salvation; he must be saved when God's Spirit convicts. John 15:16 makes it clear that it is not man's choice:

YE HAVE NOT CHOSEN ME, BUT 1 HAVE CHOSEN YOU . . .

The first question that every person should ask himself about his salvation experience 1s: 'Was my profession of faith more emotional and mental than spiritual? Did I respond to an invitation out of a deep sense of lostness or did I decide that this particular time was as good as any other? What motivated me to make the decision that I made at the time that I made it? Were there extraneous circumstances that emotionally, more than spiritually, influenced me?"

SALVATION IS DEPENDENT SOLELY UPON THE IMPUTED RIGHTEOUSNESS OF CHRIST

The tenth chapter of Romans describes Paul's burden for the Jews. In verses 1-3 of that chapter are these words:

For I bear them record that THEY HAVE A ZEAL OF GOD, but not according to knowledge. For they being ignorant of God's righteousness, and GOING
ABOUT TO ESTABLISH THEIR OWN RIGHTEOUS- NESS, have not submitted themselves unto the righteousness of God. FOR CHRIST IS THE END OF THE LAW FOR RIGHTEOUSNESS TO EVERY ONE THAT BELIEVETH.

Is it not interesting that these words are also descriptive of the membership of the modern church? Ours is a religious society that honors achievement. If we would admit it a favorite motto of manipulation is, "We are saved to serve." Terms like "work, do, attend, give, and support" are words of action that appear often in the weekly newsletter of the average evangelical church. Zealously, indeed, does the church member of today perform his allotted tasks.

Works, however, should be the fruit of salvation; they are never the root, even in part. Unwittingly, though, many who give lip-service to the grace of God are actually practicing a false salvation of works in a futile effort to find security of spirit. Romans 11:5~6 shows that grace and works cannot be blended as an agent for the securing of salvation:

Even so then at this present time also there is a remnant according to the election of grace. And if by grace, then is it no more of works: otherwise grace is no more grace. But if it be of works, then is it no more of grace: otherwise work is no more work.

Compare these verses with Paul's statement in Romans 10:4 where he asserts that "Christ is the end of the law of righteousness to every one that believeth." Salvation is not Christ plus baptism, or Christ plus the Lord's Supper, or Christ plus a good life, or Christ plus church membership, or Christ plus anything. Salvation is Christ.

I For I am not ashamed of the GOSPEL OF CHRIST: for IT IS THE POWER OF GOD UNTO SALVATION T0 EVERY ONE THAT BELIEVETH: to the Jew
first, and also to the Greek. FOR HEREIN IS THE RIGHTEOUSNESS OF GOD REVEALED FROM FAITH TO FAITH.' as it is written, THE JUST SHALL LIVE BY FAITH (Romans 1:16-17).

Man is so egotistical that it is hard for him to agree with Paul, "For I know that in me (that is, in my flesh), DWELLETH NO GOOD THING . . (Romans 7:18). The pride that permeates the nature of man refuses to make such an admission. "Surely," he says, "there is SOMETHING within me that merits God's favor." On the contrary, according to the verse just quoted, there is NOTHING within man that deserves a smile from God.

In fact, if a man could live an absolutely perfect life from the day of his birth until the day of his death, he would still go to hell if he never accepted Jesus as Lord. We need to remember that a man does not go to hell because he sins. He goes to hell because he has never been born again and is, therefore, spiritually dead. The only perfect people in your town are the people in the cemeteries. They do not lie, cheat, or steal; they are perfect, "perfectly dead." In spiritual likeness, the lost man is dead:

And you hath he quickened, who were DEAD in trespasses and sin (Ephesians 2:1).

That spiritual death was passed upon all mankind by the first Adam and his transgression. Spiritual life is granted to all who trust exclusively in God by the Lord Jesus Christ. The Scriptures share this truth in I Corinthians 15:22:

For as in Adam all die, even so in CHRIST SHALL ALL BE MADE ALIVE.

Please observe that this verse does not teach that Christ and any other human activity will bring life. Jesus Christ alone has power to save:

Neither is there salvation in any other: for THERE IS NONE OTHER NAME UNDER HEAVEN GIVEN AMONG MEN, WHEREBY WE MUST BE SAVED (Acts 4:12).

`Dr. Bailey Smith of First Southern Baptist Church of Del City, Oklahoma received widespread criticism because of a statement he made while serving as president of the Southern Baptist Convention. Dr. Smith said that God did not hear the prayer of a Jew. Newspaper columnists, civil rights activists, and the anti-defamation leagues presented Dr. Smith as a bigot of the worst sort. Technically speaking, God does hear the prayers of every- one, even mock prayer crouched in blasphemy. What Dr. Smith meant, and the Bible teaches, is that no prayer will be answered by God unless it comes through the authority of Jesus' name. The Lord Jesus states firmly in John 14:6:

I am THE way, THE truth, and THE life: NO MAN COMETH UNTO THE FATHER BUT BY ME. ,

Jesus is not a good way to heaven and He is not the best way to heaven. Jesus is the only way to heaven. If that sounds like a radical, right-wing, ultra-conservative speaking, remember that the speaker is the Lord Jesus. Our present society asks for tolerance and broadmindedness in everything. Frankly, there is a real danger of becoming so broadminded our brains fall out. The gospel has a three point aspect and is very narrow:

Moreover, brethren, I declare unto you THE GOSPEL WHICH I PREACHED UNTO YOU, which also ye have received, and wherein ye stand; BY WHICH ALSO YE ARE SAVED, if ye keep in memory what I preached unto you, unless ye have believed in vain. For I delivered unto you first of all that which I also received, HOW THAT CHRIST DIED FOR OUR SINS ACCORDING TO THE SCRIPTURES: AND THAT HE WAS BURIED: AND THAT HE ROSE AGAIN THE THIRD DAY ACCORDING TO THE

SCRIPTURES (I Corinthians 15:1-4}.

The individual seeking assurance for his salvation must ask himself, "When I made my profession, in what or whom was I trusting for salvation? Was I placing my faith in anything or anyone other than the Lord Jesus Christ and Him alone? If his trust was just one particle of faith in anything other than the Lord Jesus Christ and His shed blood, that man is still lost and is not saved.

SALVATION COMES BY CALLING UPON THE LORD

Silent and secret discipleship is an unknown phenomenon in the New Testament. More and more this generation is hearing a gospel of easy believism. Trust without oral confession has become the order of the day in evangelism. The Bible, however, emphasizes the use of open, verbal communicator. as a part of the salvation experience. Continuing in the tenth chapter of Romans, mark well these words:

But what saith it? The word is nigh thee, EVEN IN THY MOUTH, and in thy heart: that is, the word of faith, which we preach; That if THOU SHALT CONFESS WITH THY MOUTH the Lord Jesus (Christ) and shalt believe in thine heart that God hath raised him from the dead, thou shalt be saved. For with the heart man believeth unto righteousness; and WITH THE MOUTH CONFESSION IS MADE UNTO SALVATION (Romans 10:8-10).

What do these verses mean? For the sake of illustration, let us suppose that we are present at a revival service during the invitation time Two men respond b moving out into the aisles and striding quickly toward the altar. Two counselors are waiting, and each meets one of the men.

The first man kneels and listens intently as the plan of salvation is explained. With the encouragement of his counselor, he prays, "Lord be merciful to me a sinner and save my soul for Jesus' sake." When the prayer is com- pleted, his counselor asks, "Are you saved?" The answer softly returns, "I don't know; I don't think so." Was this man saved? No, according to Romans 10:8-10, he was not.

The exact same circumstances occur with the second sinner. He prays the identical words that the first man has just prayed. When asked if he is now saved, however, there is an opposite response. He exudes, "Yes, praise God, I am saved!" Was this man saved? Again, according to the verses just quoted, he was. The following verse emphasizes the importance of a vocal confession:

For the scripture saith, Whosoever believeth on him SHALL NOT BE ASHAMED (Romans 10:11).

Even more clearly presented is the admonition of the Lord Jesus Christ that his followers be ready to confess him openly before men.

Also I say unto you, WHOSOEVER SHALL CONFESS ME BEFORE MEN, HIM SHALL THE SON OF MAN ALSO CONFESS BEFORE THE ANGELS OF GOD: BUT HE THAT DENIETH ME BEFORE MEN SHALL
BE DENIED BEFORE THE ANGELS OF GOD (Luke 12:8-9).

That very plain, straightforward warning by the Lord Jesus should be accepted at face value. He will not embrace as his own any person who will not confess Him. What a horrible time it will be when multitudes of moral, religious, but silent, people find themselves cast out of the Father's presence.

Any pastor who has been in the ministry for very much time at all can relate scores of testimonies from people who responded to an invitation and were never told to invite Jesus to come into their lives and to save them. Some were told to fill out a membership card, others were congratulated for uniting with the church, and still others were baptized. Is it any wonder that these people live empty, powerless lives? We must call upon the Lord:

For whosoever shall CALL upon the name of the Lord shall be saved (Romans 10:13).

Every person who comes forward to accept Christ should be told to call upon the Lord for salvation. One of the reasons that a person may be experiencing doubts is because He never called upon God as the Bible directs.

Anyone who is wondering about his salvation should ask himself, "At the time of my profession of faith, do I remember asking Jesus Christ to save me from my sin?" If you know that you never prayed that prayer in spite of the clear command. of Romans 10:13, then you have good cause to question the fact of your conversion. However, if you prayed to Him by the quickening power of the Spirit, you can claim the blessing of Titus 1:2:

In hope of eternal File, which GOD, THAT CANNOT LIE, promised before the world began.

SALVATION BRINGS SORROW FOR COMMITTED SIN

When God saves a man, He does not put him in a place so far removed from sin that he will never indulge himself again. A Christian may sin, but when sin enters his life, the result is remorse and repentance; if his sins persist, he is forced to endure the chastisement of God. Our Lord will not allow one of His children to sin and continue living a tranquil life.

Suppose a man has spent the entire day wading through the muddy trails of a rain-drenched forest while hunting with his favorite dog. Arriving home and covered with mud from head to toe, he enters his spotless home. Without removing his trousers or boots, he whistles for his dog to join him, and together they lounge on his wife's newly-purchased sofa. If he does not hear a voice screaming at him to get that filth out of the house, what does that say about his wife? It says that she is not home! Romans 8:9 speaks of the sinless Holy Spirit that is "at home" in the believer:

But ye are not in the flesh, but in the Spirit, IF SO BE THAT THE SPIRIT OF GOD DWELL IN YOU, now IF ANY MAN HAVE NOT THE SPIRIT OF CHRIST, HE IS NONE OF HIS.

In other words, when you sin, what happens? If you do not hear the voice of the Holy Ghost reprimanding you for the sin you have brought into your life, then the Holy Ghost is not residing in your heart. The vileness of sin and the virtue of the Holy Ghost cannot peacefully dwell together. That brings us to another question that the saint who is seeking for assurance may ask himself, "Is there a difference between my life before my profession of faith and afterwards in the comfort or lack of comfort that accompanies any sin that I may commit?" If a very obvious difference exists, one may safely take confidence in the security of his salvation.

SALVATION RESULTS IN A NEW NATURE

Romans 6:6 informs us that the old nature is gone, but upon its demise a new nature begins to bloom. The precious Holy Spirit is infused into the believer's life. Such power as was never previously enjoyed leaps to energize and provide authority for every God-directed endeavor of the newly-saved individual. If we accept the Bible doctrine of the trinity as a fundamental and experiential scriptural fact, the presence of God the Holy Spirit actually means that God the Father and God the Son are also indwelling him. Each of these three have specific and different offices of function, but each possesses the human qualities of personhood, which means that their collective nature becomes the innermost nature of the Christian. In II Peter 1:2-4 are these words:

Grace and peace be multiplied unto you through the knowledge of God, and of Jesus our Lord, according as his divine power HATH GIVEN UNTO US ALL THINGS THAT PERTAIN UNTO LIFE AND GODLINESS, through the knowledge of him that hath called us to glory and virtue; by which are given unto us exceedingly great and precious promises, that by these YE MIGHT BE PARTAKERS OF THE DIVINE NATURE, having escaped the corruption that is in the world through lust.

It is an awesome thing to consider that the very infinite, almighty, eternal God of Glory can live within a man. But it is an express teaching of the Word of God that He does. That being true, what is the dominant trait of our Lord's nature? Is it love? Is it His wrath? Is it mercy? As precious as these qualities are, these are not primary. His leading attribute is His holiness.

God cannot and will not tolerate sin. The discomfort and grief suffered by the believer who sins is actually the groaning and grief of the Spirit within him. Ephesians 4:30 alludes to this grief by declaring:

And GRIEVE NOT THE SPIRIT of God whereby ye are sealed unto the day of redemption.

Let it be well understood that reformation will not bring this new nature into man's possession. The cessation of any vice (i.e. drugs, alcohol, illicit sex) will bring outward cleanliness, but man s greatest need is for inward life. Inward life comes only by spiritual regeneration.

There are two ways by which you may determine whether the new nature exists within. First, is there a sense of genuine repentance and pain whenever you transgress God's law? We have previously discussed this aspect.

The second means of determination is by examination of your hunger for God's Word. Life of any kind requires a fitting food for strength. Plants need nutrients, cattle need grain, human babies feed on milk, and Christians thirst for the Word:

As newborn babes, DESIRE THE PURE MILK OF THE WORD, that ye may grow by it (I Peter 2:2).

If. there is not a definite increase in one's appetite for Bible study following his profession of faith, it means that salvation did not occur at all. Even a lost man may possess the necessary self-discipline to eliminate so many sinful habits and addictions from his life that he may appear to _be an entirely different person. One thing he cannot do is develop spiritual appetites from an innermost part of himself when that part has never been made alive. If he finds himself craving time alone with God in prayer, looking for new insights of interpretation as he studies the Word, and feeling a sense of personal loss when not able to attend regular Bible study groups, then that man unquestionably possesses the new nature of the loving Father. He has been born again!

SALVATION IS PROVEN BY THE KEEPING OF GOD'S COMMANDMENTS

The little book of I John is especially addressed to the family of God. Its primary theme is the assurance of the believer's relationship with the Father. That theme is stated in chapter five arid verse thirteen of the book. and provides the necessary certainty of salvation:

These things have I written unto you that believe on the name of the Son of God.

John did not use terms like "ye may guess" or "ye may hope"; he said, "ye may KNOW." The old-timers conveyed the same belief with, "If you can have it and not know it, then you might lose it and never miss it!"

The first way that John presents for assurance that salvation is secure can be found in chapter two, verse three:

And by this we do KNOW that we KNOW him, if we keep his commandments.

Important to the believer's sense of well-being about his relationship to the Lord is the determination of what constitutes his first line of defense in his war against sin. Consider this illustration. A man is tempted to steal some money from his employer. Why does he choose not to do it? He might consider the embarrassment that his family would suffer if he should be discovered. He could decide that it would be unethical and immoral. He might reach the conclusion that his boss has been too supportive to be treated so shabbily in return. All of these are excellent reasons for refusing to steal. But if he instantly sees this action as a sin against God, then this man is a Christian according to the verse just quoted. The believer's first and most powerful response to the challenge of sin results from the sensitivity of the Holy Spirit indwelling him.

SALVATION IS PROVEN LOVE FOR THE CHURCH

John shares another proof of salvation's assurance in I John 3:14. Every believer should be required to spend hours of his time in prayerful meditation of the message contained in this brief passage:

We KNOW that we have passed from death unto life, because we love the brethren. He that loveth not his brother abideth in death.

"Brethren" is a word employed quite often throughout the New Testament. The word finds its greater meaning in its application to the men and women who, because of their mutual births into the family of God, are now spiritual brothers and sisters. Nothing quite matches the joy of a family reunion. Every week finds God's family having times of togetherness in fellowship around the Word. No outsider relishes the idea of going to a reunion if the family has no relationship to him. Similarly, the lost man tries to avoid group meetings of God's family, whether the meetings are in worship or in play. The people involved are not his brothers and are not his sisters. The saved man wants to be with his family.

SALVATION IS PROVEN BY SINCERE BELIEF THAT JESUS IS GOD'S SON

We will take one more passage from John's writings to prove the security of the believer. In I John 4:15 are words that declare the cardinal truth of the Christian church:

Whosoever shall confess that Jesus is the Son of God, GOD DWELLETH IN HIM, AND HE IN GOD.

The truth of this statement is validated by the conversation between Philip and the Ethiopian eunuch as recorded in Acts 8:36-38. Arguments about the exact time of an individual's salvation are settled in the account as recorded here. It was not after baptism nor after religious instruction. The eunuch was saved the moment he acknowledged by confession the identity of Christ.

And as they went on their way, they came unto a certain water; and the eunuch said, See here is water. What doth hinder me to be baptized? And Philip said, If thou believes! with all thine heart, thou mayest. And he answered and said, I BELIEVE THAT JESUS

CHRIST IS THE SON OF GOD. And he commanded the chariot to stand still; and they both went down into the water; both Philip, and the eunuch, and he baptized him. .

HOW SECURE IS SALVATION?

Most believers have considerable difficulty in fully appreciating the magnitude of God's love and protective care for all of His children. Fretting, undue anxiety, fear, nervousness, doubt, and frustration become companions to him as he moves through the complexities of this life. Many precious promises may be found in the Bible to substantiate the doctrinal position of what is often called, "eternal security," or "once saved, always saved." But one verse that fully and finally lays the issue to rest is I Peter I: 1-3, 3-5:

Blessed be God and Father of our Lord Jesus Christ, who according to his abundant mercy, hath begotten us again unto a lively hope by the resurrection of Jesus Christ from the dead, to an inheritance incorruptible, and undefiled, and that fadeth away, reserved in heaven for you, WHO ARE KEPT BY THE POWER OF GOD THROUGH FAITH UNTO SALVATION ready to be revealed in the last time.

Quite often there is opposition leveled at the one who believes in the security of the saint by the insistence that a Christian can only stay saved by rigidly adhering to a life of faithfulness. In the verse just shared, the word used is "faith," not "faithfulness." It is frequently argued that the maintenance of salvation is provided by the believer's ability to overcome the world. Overcoming the world, however, is not accomplished by faithfulness; it is a work of faith:

For WHATSOEVER IS BORN OF GOD OVERCOMETH THE WORLD: and this is the victory that over- cometh the world, EVEN OUR FAITH. Who is he that overcometh the world, but HE THAT BELIEVETH THAT JESUS IS THE SON OF GOD? (I John 5:4-5).

How amazing! The moment that salvation becomes our permanent possession, this verse declares that we will have already overcome the world. Please note, it is by our faith, not our faithfulness, that the world system is conquered! The possibility of this precious truth was as- sured and is the direct result of our Lord's high priestly prayer as recorded in the seventeenth chapter of John. In that prayer, Jesus prays:

I have given them thy ward; and the world hated them, because they are not of the world, even as I am not of the world. I pray not that thou shouldest take them out of the world, but that thou shouldest keep them from the Evil One. THEY ARE NOT OF THE WORLD, EVEN AS I AM NOT OF THE WORLD. . . . Neither pray I for these alone, BUT FOR THEM ALSO WHO SHALL BELIEVE ON ME THROUGH THEIR WORD: THAT THEY MAY BE ONE, AS THOU, FATHER, ART IN ME, AND I IN THEE, that they also may be in us; THAT THE WORLD MAY BE- LIEVE THAT THOU HAST SENT ME (John 27:14- 16. ' 20-21).

Another important word in I Peter 1:4 is "power." When this word is connected with "God," as it is here, it takes on a unique definition. One of the singular qualities of the Father is that He is omniscient (ability to know everything). omnipresent (ability to be every- where), and omnipotent (ability to do anything). Understanding this, the phrase in I Peter 1:4 develops a new meaning. Putting it together, as we have examined it thus far, we see that we are kept by a supernatural ability to do anything through a condition of faith (not our faithfulness) that is an answer to the interceding high priestly prayer of the Lord Jesus.

But what about the word, "kept"? This word is seen in other places in the New Testament. It comes from the root word in the original language that carries with it the idea of a garrison of soldiers who have the express responsibility of guarding a person or thing. One of the more familiar verses in which the word is used is in II Timothy 1:12 where commitments are secured:

For which cause I also suffer these things; nevertheless, I am not ashamed; for I know whom I have believed and am persuaded that he is able to KEEP that which I have committed unto him against that day.

Another familiar verse is Philippians 4:7. Unlike II Timothy 1:12, "keep" is used in this passage to speak of the way our very hearts and minds are protected by God's garrison:

And the peace of God, which passeth all understanding, shall KEEP your hearts and minds through Christ Jesus.

Now, remember that in I Peter 1:4 we are told that we are "kept by the power of God through faith unto salvation." We have seen that the word is in reference to an encircling garrison of protection. That garrison is identified in Psalms 125: 1-2.

They who trust in the Lord shall be as Mount Zion, which cannot be removed, but abideth forever. AS THE MOUNTAINS ARE

ROUND ABOUT JERUSALEM, SO THE LORD IS ROUND ABOUT HIS PEOPLE FROM HENCEFORTH EVEN FOREVER.

One of the saint's most incredible discoveries is that he is utterly surrounded by the Lord Himself! What a wondrous thought! We can now read I Peter 1:4 with a clearer idea of God's message to His children:

We are garrisoned about by the Lord Himself because of His ability to do anything through faith, not faithfulness, which is the result of Christ's high priestly prayer unto our salvation.

In summation, this chapter has attempted to provide the reader with concrete questions that he may ask himself concerning his spiritual experiences. These questions can settle forever the anxiety of doubts about his relationship with God. Accept for yourself that every true believer is secure in Jesus. May you grip the strength of that fact and apply it to yourself so that you also have the assurance
which is the birthright of every child of God.

PRACTICAL APPLICATIONS
for
"How to Have the Assurance of Salvation"

1. Use your concordance to find the verses in the New Testament where "believe" is used in connection with salvation. List the location of each verse below.

2. If possible, contact someone who was present when you made your profession of faith. Ask them to share in detail what happened.

Define these words:
(1)Justification

(2)Conversion

(3)Regeneration

(4)Sanctification

4. Write your personal testimony

Chapter Three

HOW TO KNOW THE WILL OF GOD

Understanding the will of God can sometimes be perplexing and has certainly been a major focal point in religious debates since the earliest days of man's initial journeys with God. Because of the mysterious qualities surrounding this great Bible doctrine, we have grown accustomed to thinking of His will for our lives in some rather unscriptural ways. For example, we speak of "finding the will of God" and yet the Bible never indicates that we must "find" it. We speak of trying to determine the "future will of God for our lives" when the Scriptures insist upon talking about the daily walk of the believer. It is obvious that such misconceptions and obscurities in definition only serve to muddle the minds of many within the Christian family.

At some point, the anxious believer needs to have some of his questions answered so that his walk in the Spirit may be filled with a new and more determined resolve. The seeking believer must make himself fully aware that God is not some heavenly tyrant with a cruel sense of humor. No father would ever tell his child to do some- thing under the promise of reward for doing it and under threat of punishment if his child did not, without first telling his child specifically what was expected of him. If he did, he would be a cruel father indeed. His poor child would be motivated to do whatever was expected in order to earn the prize, but almost mortified that should he fail, painful disciplinary action would surely follow. In answer to his most earnest pleadings for information about what his father desired, he only heard "I'm not going to tell you.

You'll have to find it. If you do, good things will be yours. If you do not find it, prepare yourself for some bad consequences."

Everyone agrees that such unusual treatment would not be that of a loving person. However, the frustration of countless Christians is testimony to the undeniable fact that the majority of those within the Body of Christ have little or no idea as to what constitutes the will of God; and, as a result, these same believers wrestle with a false image of God who is playing some sort of "theological hide-and-seek" with them.

Any serious discussion of the will of God can best begin in Romans 12: 1-2 where the Scriptures say:

I beseech ye therefore, brethren, by the mercies of God, that ye present your bodies a living sacrifice, holy, acceptable unto God, which is your reasonable service. And be not conformed to this world, but be ye transformed by the renewing of your mind, that ye may prove what is that good, and acceptable, and perfect, will of God.

Within these two verses can be found the secret of living in the will of God. In fact, the formula for knowing God's will might well be P ("present your bodies") plus T ("transform your minds") equals W ("will of God"). Simply, P+T.=W.

PRESENTATION OF THE BODY

Important to the normal Christian life is the priority and meaning, one gives to the desires of his body. The believer must decide whether he will serve his body or whether his body will serve him in his attempt to bring honor and glory to God. Therefore, the first part of the formula must be PRESENTATION OF THE BODY.

The Scriptures exhort that we are to "present our bodies a living sacrifice" (Romans 12:1). Fleshhooks held the Old Testament animals of sacrifice securely in place. If we are to sacrifice ourselves after the same type as the animal sacrifices of the Mosaic creed, we must be willing to be "tied down." A new commitment to the basics isnecessary if we would know His perfect will. The disciplines of faithful church attendance, consistent witnessing, and devotion to Bible study and prayer are essentials to the expansion of our view of what the Lord is trying to accomplish. Why should God reveal His greater will for our lives when we are not already doing the things that He has explicitly asked of us?

To illustrate, let us suppose that a man is planning a trip from New York to Los Angeles. Everything goes well until darkness begins to fall at the end of the first day. Although he feels like continuing, he decides to discontinue his trip until the next morning. His reason for failing to proceed through the darkness is his rather illogical concern that his headlamps can only shine some two hundred feet ahead of his automobile, rather than shining the entire span of the darkened road from New York to Los Angeles. What really happens, of course, is that as his automobile moves forward, the illuminated section of road in front of it moves forward by the same proportion. As we perform that segment of God's will that we clearly see, our spiritual vision moves forward to see another segment of the clearly defined will of God, that we could not previously see.

All of our Christian growth experience follows that same

order. Take note of the words of David as he gave his reasons for his belief that he could overcome Goliath. In I Samuel 17:34 are these words:

And David said unto Samuel, Thy servant kept his father's sheep, and there came a lion, and a bear, and took a lamb out of the flock; and I went out after him, and smote him, and delivered it out of his mouth . . . David said, moreover, the Lord who delivered me out of the paw of the lion, and out of the paw of the bear, he will deliver me out of the hand of this Philistine . . .

David knew the will of God about his coming conflict with Goliath because he had already been victorious in his battles with the lion and the bear. Had he refused the conflicts with the lion and bear, David would never have been brought to the position of having the necessary confidence in God so that he could predict the outcome of his forthcoming battle with the giant.

This combines very well with Romans 12:3 which speaks of this same progressive growth in God-and-man consciousness, called faith:

For I say, through the grace given unto me, to every man that is among you, not to think of himself more highly than he ought to think, but to think soberly, according as GOD HATH DEALT TO EVERY MAN THE MEASURE or FAITH.

Billy Graham began his ministry in some obscure, almost forgotten meeting scores of years ago. It would have been absurd to have whisked Graham instantly from that quaint little meeting to the pulpit of one of his gigantic crusades. He was not ready. A step by step growth process was necessary as his measure of faith increased.

Even so, no believer can ever know the great, "abstract" will of God until he disciplines his body to do those things he may not necessarily be inclined‘ to do. The sacrificial aspect of our journey with Christ mandates that we be absolutely willing to place ourselves in whatever position on the altar of living sacrifice that He may choose.

TRANSFORMATION OF THE MIND

In our formula for knowing the will of God, the "T" stands for "transformation of minds." Transformation comes from the same root word as metamorphosis. A brief recollection of elementary biology will remind you that metamorphosis is the process that occurs by which a caterpillar becomes abutterfly. Please note that in Romans 12:2 that very same kind of dramatic change is required in our minds, very probably because of the already existent fact of II Corinthians 5:17:

Therefore, if any man be in Christ, he is a new creature; old things are passed away; behold, all things are become new.

But II Corinthians 5:17 has to do with man's spirit. Salvation can instantly transform man's spirit; man's mind requires a much slower process. Romans 12:2 calls it renewal.

The word "renew," actually means "a new, a different, way." Since according to Romans 6:6, the old man is dead, and since according to II Corinthians 5:17, a new man has been created, it only stands to reason that the old mind food which had previously been fed into the mind will not suffice; for the mind to be as transformed as the spirit, there must be new mind food. Quality selectivity in terms of choices for reading and seeing and listening is very important.

Never has a world been so bombarded with a myriad of sights and sounds. It is estimated that the average American will be confronted by over 1600 advertisements every single day. This profusion of intentionally designed creations for the development of some desire within the human mind bears a note of foreboding for even the most skeptical of believers. The record industry has been guilty of concealing some of its more subliminal suggestions with the use of a relatively new technique called "backward masking." Consumable items, particularly foods, are packaged in colors that have been psychologically tested for their abilities to appeal to man's natural hunger for sweet, sour, and etc.

Recognizing the fact that there is an almost constant stream of commercial and philosophical ideas being pumped into his eyes and ears during every waking hour, the wise believer will make himself aware of the more flagrant un-Christlike intrusions. Otherwise, a spiritual callousness will occur that desensitizes him to the awfulness of sin. Modern Christian families allow pornographic scenes and profane language to enter their homes by way of the television. In previous generations, such perverse actions and unholy performances would have been shocking and forbidden. But, you see, we have been numbed by the frequency of sin.

It is not enough, however, to screen the undesirable elements from our minds. We must also feed the thoughts into it. A good rule to follow is found in Philippians 4:8:

Finally, brethren, whatsoever things are true, whatsoever things are honest, whatsoever things are just, whatsoever things are lovely, whatsoever things are of good report; if there be any virtue, and if there be any praise, THINK ON THESE THINGS.

You must understand that you are instructed not to be conformed to the world but to be transformed. Conformity to the world means a blending in with the world. The distinguishing marks of the Christian life seem to fade and a likeness to the world emerges when an individual conforms to the expectations of 'those who love the world. You begin to look, act, and sound like the people around you. Like the camouflage clothing of the military, that with its multi-colored splotches perfectly matches the colors of the surroundings, many weak believers find themselves becoming more and more like the world. The only way not to be conformed to the world is by transforming (metamorphosizing) your mind.

The same root word from which we get transform and metamorphosis is also the word from which we get the word "transfigure." In Mark 9:2 are these words:

And after six days Jesus taketh with him Peter, and James, and John, and leadeth them up into an high mountain, apart by themselves; and he was TRANSFIGURED before them.

This scene from the transfiguration of Jesus is actually what the Lord is asking of each believer in Romans 12: 1-2. Transfiguration, like transformation and metamorphosis means the outward demonstration or manifestation of that which dwells within." Before His transfiguration, Christ had so well-concealed His divinity within the body of His humanity that even His disciples had been unable to see clearly the God who was among them. Neither can the lost world see the God who lives within us unless we purposely metamorphosis, transfigure, transform our- selves. The filling of our minds with Christ-honoring materials will automatically force from our minds that which is of the flesh.

UNDERSTANDING HIS WILL

After the believer has presented his body as a living sacrifice and has transformed himself by the renewing of his mind, the will of God for his life will be revealed. However, the revelation of God's will does not necessarily mean that the struggle is over. Please note that after following the P+'I=W formula, the discovered will of God is "the good, and acceptable, and perfect will of God." Does this imply that there is another kind of God's will?

THE PERMISSIVE WILL

Yes, it does. But the other aspect of the will of God is decidedly inferior to the one listed above. We sometimes hear the other one called the "permissive will of God." A good example of God's permissive will is found in the story of the prophet-, Balaam. Balaam is approached by the pagan king, Balak, and is asked by him to place a curse upon the children of Israel. God tells Balaam to refuse. When Balaam reports God's reply to Balak, Balak offers the prophet a bribe to concur. Again, God refuses the request of Balaam. Eventually, after frequent pleadings by Balaam, God reluctantly allows the prophet to do as he wishes but curses him in the process. Although he permitted Balaam to do as he wished, He did not endorse it. It was His permissive will.

Balaam's transgression in persuading God to relinquish to his very selfish petitions became a badge of dishonor. His name will forever be associated with the false teachers of the ages. In Jude ll can be found a reference to this man's folly and God's view of it:

Woe unto them! For they have gone in the way of Cain, AND RAN GREEDILY AFTER THE ERROR OF BALAAM FOR REWARD, and perish in gainsaying of Korah.

His sin proves an interesting point. Sometimes there is a curse attached to answered prayer. We do not ordinarily associate persistent prayer with anything but blessing, but the account of Balaam as he repeatedly returned to God with a stubborn and unbent will shows that there are times, isolated and few as they may be, that God yields to what we may consider are the foolish whims and sinful purposes of a man. The Lord sets in motion His permissive will.

Probably the most striking example of the curse of answered prayer, which actually thwarts the perfect will Of God, is found in the eleventh chapter of the Book of Numbers. The people of Israel had been led by their liberator, Moses, from the bondage of servitude in Egypt to the freedom provided by the miraculous crossing of the Red Sea. Yet, in the wilderness, free from oppression and fed well by the provision of manna from heaven, they began complaining bitterly because of the lack of meat. Ingratitude was a rampant condition. Spawned by dissatisfaction, their vocal discontentment must have spread like wild fire until finally a showdown between the people and Moses occurred. The following verses vividly capture their rebelliousness

And the mixed multitude fell to lusting, and the children of Israel also wept again, and said, WHO SHALL GIVE US FLESH TO EAT? We remember the flesh which we did eat in Egypt freely; the cucumbers, and the melons, and the leeks, and the onions, and the garlic. BUT NOW OUR SOUL IS DRIED AWAY: THERE IS NOTHING AT ALL, BESIDES THIS MANNA, BEFORE OUR EYES (Numbers 11:4-6).

THEN MOSES HEARD THE PEOPLE WEEP THROUGHOUT THEIR FAMILIES, EVERY MAN IN THE DOOR OF HIS TENT: AND THE ANGER OF THE LORD WAS KINDLED GREATLY. Moses also was displeased. And Moses said unto the Lord, wherefore hast thou afflicted thy servant . . . from where should I have flesh to give unto all this people? FOR THEY WEEP UNTO ME, SAYING, GIVE US FLESH, THAT WE MAY EAT. I am not able to bear all this people alone, because it is too heavy for me (Numbers I.l:I0- II, 13-14)

What pathetic pettiness! Spoiled and childish, these Israelites resorted to begging, actually demanding, God to give them meat. Remember, it was not God's perfect will for them to have the meat. The kind of will described earlier in this chapter was not important to the children of Israel. For one thing, they were not about to present their bodies a living sacrifice as stipulated in Romans 12:1-2. They wanted meat, and God had better give it to them!

Don't ever be guilty of saying that God does not have a sense of humor! With the wisdom that only He possesses, the Lord answers the bothersome requests of the people by not just granting their wish for meat, but REALLY GRANTING THEIR WISH FOR

MEAT:

And say thou unto the people, Sanctify yourselves for tomorrow, AND YE SHALL EAT FLESH: FOR 'YE HAVE WEPT IN THE EARS OF THE LORD, Saying, who shall give us flesh to eat? For it was well with us in Egypt; therefore THE LORD WILL GIVE YOU FLESH, AND YE SHALL EAT. Ye shall not eat one day, nor two days, nor five days, neither ten days, nor twenty days; BUT EVEN A WHOLE MONTH, UNTIL IT COME OUT AT YOUR NOSTRIL5, AND IT BE LOATHSOME UNTO YOU: because ye have despised the Lord who is among you, and have wept before him, saying, Why came we forth out of Egypt? (Numbers 11:18-20).

How often we are guilty of forcing God into invoking His permissive will when that was not His perfect plat: at all! An innumerable number of young ladies have to d their pastors of the woeful marriages they have endured because they married the wrong men. Why did they make the wrong choices? So often it was the result of a resolute determination to have that person whether God approved or not. The poor love-struck girl continued plaguing God until He relented. And she will forever after rue the day that God did allow her, by His permission, to make that tragic mistake.

THE PRINCIPLE OF "I AM: I WILL"

Assuming that the believer has been able to fully incorporate for himself the formula given at the first of this chapter for discerning the will of God (P+T=W), and assuming that he has discounted as much as he can the permissive will of God, what is the most important attribute of our Lord for him to consider? The

assurance
and peace of relaxing in God's perfect will is made real by understanding who He is and what He intends to do. You will remember that our Lord has always had a preference in answering the question of who He is by saying, "I Am!" With that appellation He is saying of Himself, "There is nothing that has ever happened, is now happening, or will ever happen that will catch me unprepared. I know the end from the beginning and can bring my own 'present tense vitality' to any problem faced by any of my followers." Capture the strength of promise for all of us found in this verse:

Behold, I AM the Lord, the God of all flesh; IS THERE ANYTHING TOO HARD FOR ME? (Jeremiah 32:27).

A lesson that all of us could better learn is that "because God is, He will; since we aren't, we can't." That just about sums it up! Relying upon Him and trusting Him completely can open new dimensions of adventures in faith. Continuing in the thirty-second chapter of Jeremiah are these words:

And they shall be my people, and I WILL be their God; and I WILL give them one heart, and one way, that they may fear me forever, for the good of them, and of their children after them; And I WILL make an everlasting covenant with them, that I WILL not turn away from doing them good, but I WILL put my fear in their hearts, that they shall not depart from me. Yea, I WILL rejoice over them in doing them good, and I WILL plant them in this land assuredly with my whole heart and my whole soul. For thus saith the Lord, As I have brought all this great evil upon this people, so WILL I bring upon them all the good that I have promised them (Jeremiah 32:38-42).

God keeps saying, "1 am, I will!" Our sole responsibility is to position ourselves as recipients of all that God wants to give us. The fundamental flaw of self-effort is the opposite of "I am - I will"; it is "I am not — I cannot." Therefore. the stream of power for living is found within the channel of God's perfect will, which like the tracks of a railroad, has a definite and pre-determined destination. When off the track of His will and venturing down the paths of self-choosing, the believer heads toward an uncertain earthly destiny with the journey passing through a world system characterized by multitudes of dangerous pitfalls. By following the requirements discussed in the earlier pages of this chapter, by avoiding His permissive will resulting from the curse of answered prayer, and by knowing the principle of "I am — I will," a believer can face life confidently in the perfect will of God!

PRACTICAL APPLICATIONS
for
"How to Know the Will of God"

1. List ten specific things God asks of you right now. You may
   already be doing them.

(1)

(2)

(3)

(4)

(5)

(6)

(7)

(8)

(9)

(10)

2. What are you doing with your life that is distinctively Christian?

3. Recall and list three times that you missed the will of God in a given situation. Tell why it happened.

(1)

(2)

(3)

4. Decide what thoughts via books, plays, speeches, music, etc. you plan to start feeding into your mind. List what you consider are five of the more important.

(1)

(2)

(3)

(4)

(5)

Chapter Five

How To Overcome Temptations

The journey of the believer can be quite treacherous, and that journey only begins at salvation. In fact, the acceptance of Jesus Christ as Savior brings the recipient into a new dimension of spiritual warfare. He is besieged by temptations that he never believed would trouble him at all. His success in his quest for spiritual victory and maturity, as well as his own salvation, will be largely dependent upon his ability to recognize temptations and overcome them rather than being overcome by them. The object of this chapter will be to address the pitfalls of temptations and clearly show how they may be bridged.

We need to understand that the children of God are caught right in the middle of an on-going "spiritual tug-of-war." On the one side we are being pulled by the Spirit of God toward a life of dependence on God; on the other side we are being drawn by the world toward a dependence on self. The world charms the believer by urging him to deny God and. in so doing, become a rugged individualist who has "pulled himself up by his own bootstraps." That was precisely the problem of Esau's attitude toward life that resulted in God's pronouncement of an eternal curse upon him and his family (Malachi 1:1-3). The world says, "You can do your own thing," and, "If it feels good. do it." But God says,

Love not the world, neither the things that are in the world. If any man love the world, the love of the Father is not in him (I John 2:15).

Clearly, then, the Scriptures teach that the choice of serving God or the world is a decision that confronts every believer. Let me emphasize again that the battle does not cease when one is saved. Hundreds of times and with an untold number of disguises, the believer will be challenged by the Evil One again and again after he has been born again.

The most difficult aspect of this struggle is in determining whether a given situation is a temptation or an opportunity. Even the most immature saint can easily recognize a situation that is obviously wrong. Unfortunately, however, most of the believer's warfare with the world will be waged in shady areas that are "gray," neither white nor black. How confusing! We want so desperately to do that which honors God, but we cannot always easily determine that which is God-honoring, as opposed to that which is world-conforming. Is it a temptation or is it an opportunity? Is it of God, or is it of the world?

We do not have to wonder! The Lord tells us in I John 2:16:

For all that is in the world, the lust of the flesh, the lust of the eyes, and the pride of life, is not of the Father, but is of the world.

Note how that verse begins. . . for *all* that is in the world . . That phrase means that whatever follows will comprise everything with which the saint will contend. That being true, we can now understand what the Bible means when it says about Jesus that He was "tempted in all points like as we are and yet without sin" (Hebrews 4: 15). The three areas of the world listed in I John 2:16 are the same three areas with which Jesus did battle in the fourth chapter of Matthew. Look again at I John 2:14 and note "all that is in the world." They are:

(1) "lust of the flesh"
(2) "lust of the eyes"
(3) "pride of life"

Before we analyze the methods Jesus used in warding off these three forms of attack, we must first understand what they represent. Remember, every temptation that the world can launch against us must pass through one of these three elements just listed.

THE THREE AREAS OF COMBAT

"Lust of the flesh" is that area of our lives that is dominated by the normal physical desires which God has given every member of the human race. Such desires as the need for food, drink, and sexual satisfaction are included in this grouping. There is absolutely nothing wrong with such human desires. They are, as previously mentioned, God-given. Satan attempts to corrupt the satisfaction of bodily hungers by enticing us to satisfy them through illegitimate and disobedient means. Let me give you an example. An overweight person is hungry. That is a legitimate desire. He is tempted to eat a drooling piece of hot fudge cake, but that is an illegitimate means of satisfaction. Lusts of the flesh, then, are the seductive suggestions of Satan to satisfy normal bodily desires in Christ-dishonoring ways.

"Lust of the eyes" is that area of our lives that is dominated by emotion and will. It is generally marked by an inordinate desire to acquire the things of this
world as tangible proof of our position and rank. New houses, new

cars, more elaborate jewelry, more money and scores of other material objects become the elusive stepping stones to worldly recognition.

"Pride of life" is that area of our lives that is marked by an internal drive "to be." We want to be everything from a high school quarterback to a corporate executive, from a homecoming queen to a career woman's career woman. No price is too great and no sacrifice is too painful for the attainment of whatever position we covet.

WHO BEARS THE RESPONSIBILITY FOR SIN ?

Having now established the three areas of combat, it is vital that we be fully aware of Satan's involvement. Of course, he is our ultimate enemy, even if he presents himself in other than direct frontal attacks. However, in spite of the fact that Satan does possess great power as the "Prince of the Power of the Air" (Ephesians 2:2), he cannot cause the believer to sin. Two passages confirm this by stating:

Greater is he that is in you than he that is in the world (I John 4:4).

And

But every man is tempted, when he is drawn away of HIS OWN LUST, and enticed. Then when lust hath conceived, it bringeth forth sin: and sin, when it is finished, bringeth forth death (James 1:14).

Please note that a man is "drawn away of his own lust." Satan can no more cause the believer to sin than Jesus can cause the believer to do right. Satan will, however, provide the wherewithal by which the temptation can be turned into an act of sin. For example, if a man develops a desire for alcoholic satisfaction, Satan will most assuredly provide the bottle. The final responsibility for the commission of the sin, however, rests totally upon the believer.

Since there is no way, therefore, that a man can justify his wayward actions by shifting the blame to another, even one as powerful as Satan, it becomes increasingly important for him to find God's way of escape. As I Corinthians 10:13 affirms,

There hath no temptation taken you but as is common to man: but God is faithful, who will not suffer you to be tempted above that ye are able, but will, with the temptation, also make a way to escape, that ye may be able to bear it.

So, there's the promise, and a magnificent one indeed! For God to be faithful, and Titus 1:2 says that He cannot lie, there must be at least one exit, one means of escape, for any temptation that will ever confront the believer.

THE METHOD USED BY JESUS TO OVERCOME TEMPTATION

Earlier we alluded to the temptations of Jesus as recorded in Matthew, chapter four. Is it possible that He dealt with the three areas of the world's temptations, (i.e. "the lust of the flesh, the lust of the eyes, and the pride of life")? Is it also possible that every believer can follow His example? The answer to both questions is an emphatic, "Yes!"

Someone might argue that since Jesus was also God as well as man, His power to overcome evil sets an impossible pattern for man to follow. He was, and is, God! Let there be no question about that! As God, Christ could have totally annihilated the devil, but He chose not to do so. Why? Very simply, Christ was attempting to leave for man a strategy for facing the temptations of the world. Therefore, He laid His divinity aside and in His humanity demolished the attacks of Satan. In so doing, He was, in essence, saying to every believer, "Follow me! Respond as I responded! You don't have to fall! You can be victorious! Follow me!"

Christ': battle plan was really rather basic. He used the Word! The writer of Hebrews tells us,

For the Word of God, is quick, and powerful, and sharper than any two-edged sword, piercing even to the dividing asunder of soul and spirit, and of the joints and marrow, and is a discerner of the thoughts and intents of the heart (4:12).

Christ, in His humanity, adeptly wielded the Word of God with three great sweeps. Let's study them.

First, how did Jesus deal with "lust of the flesh"? That temptation formed itself in Matthew 4:3, "And when the tempter came to him, he said, 'If thou be the Son of God. command that these stones be made bread.'" Do you see the subtlety of this demonic suggestion? Surely there could be nothing at all wrong with the eating of bread. But remember, Jesus was on a spiritual mission! What may have been acceptable in other places was totally unacceptable here!

Now that we are seeing these challenges to our Lord unfold, it must be inserted at this point that man is a trichotomous being; that is, he is body, soul, and spirit (I Thessalonians 5:23). THIS IS VERY IMPORTANT! The means by which temptations come are through these three vehicles: the world, the flesh, and the devil. And each of these vehicles will attack a particular part of man's triune being. NOW READ CAREFULLY! The lust of the flesh through the vehicle of the flesh will attack the body of man. The lust of the eyes through the vehicle of the world will attack the soul (i.e. emotions, personality) of man. The pride of life through the vehicle of the devil will attack the spirit of man. Read this paragraph again until you understand it thoroughly.

To illustrate, let us return to the scene of Christ's temptations. The lust of the flesh (the illegitimate satisfaction of a normal desire) through the vehicle of the flesh ("turn the stones to bread) is attacking His body. How does Christ counterattack? He uses His sword, the Word of God! He Says. "IT IS WRITTEN man shall not live by bread alone, but by every word that proceedeth out of the mouth of God" (Matthew 4:4) He quotes Scripture and defeats the devil!

We now move to phase two in the devil's arsenal. Lust of the flesh failed. Lust of the eyes will now be employed. There are many decent, virtuous people who succumb to lusts of the flesh. Never will they give themselves to moral licentiousness tawdry conduct and impurity of the body. Yet some of these same honest' people are morally and spiritually toppled through lusts of the eyes.' Lust of the eyes (the wrongful desire for material object) through the vehicle of the world (the attitude and philosophy of life held by those outside Christ's kingdom) attacks Christ s soul (His emotions and personality):

Again, the devil taketh him up into an exceedingly high mountain, and showeth him all the kingdoms of the world, and the glory of them. And he saith unto him, all these things will I give thee, if thou will fall down and worship me (Matthew 4:8-9).

How does Christ respond? Again He resorts to His Faithful sword by quoting the Scriptures, "Get thee hence Satan; FOR IT Is WRITTEN, Thou shalt worship the 'hi' God. and him only shalt thou serve" (Matthew 4:8-9)

Phase three, which in our Lord's experience was second, is the pride of life. This is the most serious of the three Satanic attacks because the believer comes into direct contact with his archenemy, the devil. Pride of life (a wrongful desire to be elevated to a position of social importance) through the vehicle of the devil attacks that third and innermost part of man — his spirit. The spirit of man is that part of man with which God has communion. The question of the challenge is "Is God's reputation or my own reputation the more important consideration in my life? Am I more concerned with the applause and acclaim of men for myself, or am I willing to forego the praise that could be mine in order that the Father might receive it?"

In Matthew 4:5, Satan issued the temptation of pride of life toward Jesus:

Then the devil taketh him up into the holy city, and setteth him on a pinnacle of the temple. And saith unto him, if thou be the

Son of God, cast thyself down; for it is written, he shall give his angels charge concerning thee, and in their hands they shall bear thee up, lest at any time thou dash thy foot against a stone.

Satan knew that Jesus was aware that the Jews were looking for a wonder-working Messiah. If Jesus could be persuaded to float earthward from the temple's highest point, Satan knew that those Jews at the temple site would fall in homage to their messiah. Moreover, in so doing, Jesus by his "slight" transgression would fail in the sinlessness of His redemptive mission. Satan's sinister scheme did not succeed. Again, Jesus reaches for His sword, the Word of God: "IT IS WRITTEN again, thou shalt not tempt the Lord thy God" (Matthew 4:7).

Please note that in each of the three areas of our Lord's temptations He always quoted Scripture. Three times He said, "It is written." Think about it! As God, every word that fell from His lips were in actuality as much the Word of God as were the written words of the Bible of his day, the works of the Old Testament. Yet, for the benefit of the believer, Jesus chose to quote the written Word. That, in effect, places God's stamp of endorsement on the power of the Scriptures. It means that as we intellectually consume its words, the Bible will provide the cutting' edge so vital in severing from us the tentacles of temptations.

HOW EACH KIND OF TEMPTATION ATTACKS A DIFFERENT STAGE IN THE BELEIVERS LIFE

Human experiences suggest that lust of the flesh, lust of the eyes, and pride of life, though often overlapping, seem to. have a particular power at various stages of the believers life. This explains differences in the types of pin in the life of the elderly as opposed to those of the young.

Lust of the flesh is most generally a problem faced by the teenage believer. His body is alive in ways that he has never previously experienced and will probably never experience again. Chemical and hormonal changes are resulting in almost uncontrollable surges of energy that accentuate various physical desires. Moreover, he is subjected to a veritable barrage of external influences demanding his conformity to an alien social environment that is created and supported by peer pressure. Temptations to indulge himself in smoking, drinking, sex, and drugs will never be more frequent or intense.

How does the young believer withstand it all? He follows the example of Jesus and reaches for his sword, The Word of God. He might use this verse: "Flee youthful lusts" (II Timothy 2:22). Now, like Jesus, he can assert with authority, "For it is written, 'Flee youthful lusts.' " He should not stand and fight. He should not try to be a witness. He should not try to reform his friends. Lusts of the flesh are handled best by scriptural flight. A wise person once said, "If you don't want to fall, don't stand in a slippery place."

Lust of the eyes is most generally a problem for the middle-aged. The believer is married and is usually quite firmly implanted in the work relationship that he will maintain for the rest of his life. At this point, material success and social position begin to look more and more attractive. The world launches its attack. More hours at the office can bring flashier automobiles, bigger boats, more elegant wardrobes, and status - above all, material status. How does the believer in his mid-life contend with this allurement of the world?

Like Jesus, he reaches for his sword, the Word of God, and perhaps uses I John 2:15 to assert, "It is written, love not the world, 'neither the things that are in the world . . ." As he puts more of himself into the things of light, the things of darkness will lose their attraction. That is really what our Lord meant when He said, in Matthew 10:39, "He that findeth his life shall lose it; and he that loseth his life for my sake shall find it."

Pride of life can reach its most awful peak in its manifestation to the elderly believer. Perhaps he is in a nursing home. He cannot even control his own bodily functions. His health is gone, his finances depleted, and his friends never come for visits anymore. Only occasionally, on special days, do his relatives send a card or call. Depressed in spirit, he is an easy target for Satan.

Remember! Pride of life is the medium through which the devil himself can best attack. Satan has always been an accuser. He accused God before Eve and Job before God. The elderly believer, forsaken by so many in this world, is made to wonder if perhaps God has also forsaken him. Can it be that after all these years of faithful service God really does not care?

What can the elderly believer do to turn back this attack? Again, he may follow the example of Jesus and reach for his sword, the Word of God. A verse for this temptation is James 4:7. He can, with bold authority affirm: "It is written, submit yourselves, therefore, to God. Resist the devil, and he will flee from you."

POSITIONAL CHRISTIANITY IN WARFARE

We have now discussed the Bible-based ways to deal with

the three areas of combat in temptations. Each line of defense is only as strong as the believer's faith in the authority of God's Word and his willingness to faithfully perform it. He must appropriate to himself a working knowledge of his own unique position in Christ and fight the enemy from the vantage point of that position. The vast majority of believers are easy targets of Satan be- cause of their ignorance concerning positional Christianity.

Whenever sin attacks, regardless of which temptation is employed, the first thing the believer should remember is Romans 6:6. In that verse, there is SOMETHING TO KNOW:

Knowing this, that our old man is crucified with him, that the body of sin might be destroyed, that henceforth we should not serve sin.

Every believer needs to accept as fact, even if he does not understand it completely, that his old sinful nature has been crucified.

The nature of the old man so taints even the good efforts of an unsaved person that his noble deeds become a stench in the nostrils of God. Proverbs 15:8 solemnly declares:

The sacrifice of the wicked is an abomination to the Lord.

Please note that the Lord is talking about the good things a lost man does, not the bad deeds of the flesh. This is reiterated in Isaiah 64:6:

But we are all as an unclean thing, and ALL OUR

RIGHTEOUSNESSES are as filthy rags.

These verses clearly teach that God regards everything a man does prior to his salvation as sin. If a lost man tithes his income, if a lost woman takes a bowl of hot soup to a sick neighbor, or if a lost teenager helps an old lady across an intersection, God calls it sin. How can this be?

Suppose a father is going away for a day. He calls his son to the garage and says, "I will be gone all day. I want you to wash the car for me. There are other things that I need you to do in the house and yard, but I do not want you to do any of them until you wash the car. It is more important that you get the car clean than it is that you do anything else!"

The father leaves. When he returns, to his dismay, the car is still unwashed. A confrontation follows during which the son defends himself by saying, "I know that I did not wash the car; but, Dad, I mowed the lawn, I painted the eaves, I vacuumed the carpets, and I washed the windows."

To this argument, the father sternly replies, "I made it quite clear what I wanted you to do. The time you spent doing good things should have been spent doing the best thing!"

So it is with the lost man's deeds. Time spent in charitable activities should have been spent doing that which God wants most.

Jesus said unto him, Thou shalt love the Lord, thy God, with all thy heart, and with all thy soul, and with all thy mind. THIS IS THE FIRST AND GREAT

COMMANDMENT.

If this is the greatest commandment, then the greatest sin is the failure to comply with it. Whatever time is spent doing other things is time spent out of the will of God. Therefore, whatever a lost man does is tainted by the sin of his old nature.

If you are to develop sufficient skills in overcoming temptation, you must KNOW THAT THE OLD NATURE IS CRUCIFIED WITH CHRIST. Since the time of your salvation experience, you are no longer judged for being in a continual state or condition of sin; instead, you are now judged for specific sins, whether they are good or bad (II Corinthians 5:10). The decision of what you do, as previously discussed in this chapter, is now completely in your hands. Because the old contaminating nature is dead, no longer is everything in your life stained by sin. YOU MUST KNOW THIS!

Second, your positional warfare relationship requires SOMETHING T0 RECKON. "Reckon" is a bookkeeping term which means to examine carefully the pros and cons, the assets and the liabilities. Romans 6:11 declares:

Likewise RECKON ye yourselves to be dead indeed unto sin, but alive unto God through Jesus Christ our Lord.

This verse exhorts us to place the desirable activity under scrutiny to determine whether it is a temptation or an opportunity. That evaluation is accomplished by recognizing the death of the old nature as fact and the acknowledgment of the creation of new life in Christ. It is now possible to turn the light of the mind of Christ, which is within you, upon the moral rightness and Godly acceptance or rejection of the activity. This reckoning gives the final answer for abstaining or participating.

Third, your final step is SOMETHING TO YIELD. By acting upon what you know and what you have reckoned, you can now actively involve your entire self in the over- coming of whatever temptation is being faced. Romans 6:13 says:

Neither yield ye your members as instruments of unrighteousness to sin: but YIELD YOURSELVES UNTO GOD, as those that are alive from the dead, AND YOUR MEMBERS AS INSTRUMENTS OF RIGHTEOUSNESS UNTO GOD.

AN ILLUSTRATION OF OVERCOMING A TEMPTATION

Remember, God always provides a way of escape. As previously discussed, Satan attempts to pervert legitimate natural desires by satisfying them in illegitimate ways. An illustration of this three-step positional procedure can clarify what is meant by:

(l) Knowing (Romans 6:6);
(2) Reckoning (Romans 6: 11);
(3) Yielding (Romans 6: 13)

We spoke earlier of an overweight person being tempted by a delicious hot fudge cake. To overcome this temptation he first quotes an appropriate verse as directed in this chapter about temptations of the flesh. He may choose to use the same verse that Christ employed:

It is written, man shall not live by bread alone, but by every ward that proceedeth from the mouth of God.

Next, he KNOWS THAT HIS SIN NATURE IS CRUCIFIED. He is not forced by that old nature to eat the hot fudge cake. He also RECKONS WITH JESUS and himself about the propriety of enjoying the dessert. His body is asked, "Do you want the cake?" Of course, the body's answer is in the affirmative! Christ, who lives within is asked the same question but His reply is entirely different, "N0, don't eat the cake, but eat some fresh fruit instead." He always provides a better way when He is forced to reject an unprofitable way. That is where YIELDING OURSELVES TO THE CHRIST-APPROVED WAY brings the final victory in the struggle with temptation.

In this chapter, we have covered a great deal of material. For many readers, this has been revolutionary and perplexing. Read carefully the sections not clearly understood and ask the Spirit for guidance. Temptations need not ever destroy the believer by enticing him into disobedience.

In summary, the world presents its temptations through three mediums — lust of the flesh, lust of the eyes and pride of life. Dust of the flesh is directed at man's body through the vehicle of the flesh, is a sin of the young, and is best countered by use of appropriate Scriptures. Lust of the eyes is directed at man's soul through the vehicle of the world, is a sin of the middle-aged, and is best countered by use of appropriate Scriptures. Pride of life is directed at man's spirit through the vehicle of the devil, is a sin of the elderly, and is best countered by use of appropriate Scriptures.

Temptation is not sin; it leads to sin. There is no possible way to avoid the dilemma of ever-present temptations. However, Christ has given us a plan and an example. As God's Word becomes a more integral part of our life, we will find resources of spiritual power sufficient for the battle, whatever form it may take. And regardless of Satan's sneering threats, the victory is already ours through Jesus Christ our Lord.

PRACTICAL APPLICATIONS
for
"How to Overcome Temptations" .

1. Recall from your own experience two temptations that have caused you the most anxiety. Find a verse in the Bible that you may use to defend yourself against each of these attacks. In the space below, list the two temptations and write out the verse in full.

(1)

(2)

2. Do a study from your secular dictionary, Bible dictionary, and concordance about temptations. Write 'your own definition resulting from that study.

3. List the greatest victories over temptation that you have experienced.

(1)

(2)

(3)

(4)

(5)

4. Read Christ's high priestly prayer in the seventeenth chapter of John. Find reasons for victory over temptations and write one paragraph concerning them.

Chapter Five

HOW TO PRAY FOR AN UNSAVED LOVED ONE

The most vital of relationships is that which exists between man and his Creator. As in all other personal relationships, communication is the tie that binds. Without it, any real intimacy with the God of Glory is absolutely impossible, and without that special closeness, the believer is left groping through a darkened and antagonistic world. Even as he neared the end of his glorious life and ministry, Paul is found crying with hungry desperation:

That I may know him, and the power of his resurrection, and the fellowship of his sufferings, being made conformable unto his death (Philippians 3:10).

Let it be clearly understood that very little can be written on the matter of prayer than has not already been done by countless authors, poets, and hymnwriters. Probably no aspect of the Christian experience has been more analyzed and discussed than prayer. Bookstores are over stocked with books on intercessory prayer, confessional prayer, charismatic prayer, conversational prayer, Biblical prayer (as if there is some other kind), motivational prayer, transcendental prayer, meditational prayer, healing prayer, prosperity-assuring prayer, children's prayer, students' prayer, athletes' prayer, etc. With such an abundance of materials on the subject, and so many varied perspectives, why on earth should anyone attempt to write anything, even one chapter, on such an obviously well-covered theme?

From personal experiences in the realm of spiritual warfare, it has become increasingly evident that the power of prayer has never been more potent than in the struggle for souls. By and large, this chapter will address itself to a more effective use of this powerful spiritual weapon which has been instrumental in the release of damned and deluded souls from the snares of Satan.

We will begin our study of prayer's potential by looking at the PRINCIPLE OF THE HEDGE OF THORNS. In Hosea 2:6 are these words, "Therefore, behold, I will hedge up thy way with thorns . . The story that precedes this verse is tragic. Hosea, the man of God, marries a woman whose name is Gomer. Children are born to the union. Nevertheless, one day, Gomer leaves Hosea and enters into a life of prostitution and immorality. Poor Hosea is heartsick. His plaintive cry and sense of personal violation are experiences familiar to untold thousands of spouses and parents who have repeatedly asked themselves about a wandering loved one, "Where did I go wrong? What happened? What can I do?"

Our first step toward retrieving a backslidden acquaintance from the grip of the world or an unsaved loved one from the clutches of the devil is to clearly understand that we have only two spiritual weapons. The bondage of sin cannot be broken by the reasoning of logic, by the argument of common sense, by the tears of love, by the remorse of tragedy, by the passage of years, by the threatening of discipline, by the fear of hell, by the hope of heaven, by the reformation of attitudes, by the education of minds, by the change of environments, or by any other method that man has devised or shall yet devise. Only two weapons are "mighty to the pulling down of strongholds" — prayer and the Word of God!

Undoubtedly, 'Hosea realized that any attempt by him to extricate Gomer from the entanglements of her world would be futile unless his ways were really God's ways. The world system she had entered was under the dominion and power of Satan. The best and most ingenious of human efforts will always fail when pitted against even the simplest of Satan's plans.

Knowing this, Hosea turns to the power of his spiritual arsenal. Without doubt, this man of God was fully aware of the identity of his enemy. He recognized, as Paul would say much later, that our struggle is not with flesh and blood. It is quite conceivable that Hosea spent long hours in prayerful meditation of the Word as he pondered his strategy and developed his plan by which Satan's scheme could possibly be foiled.

From somewhere, perhaps from Job 1:10, a vision of the hedge of thorns came flooding into his mind. Quickly, Hosea laid his groundwork, prepared his heart, instituted his plan, and ultimately received his wife to himself again.

What the hedge of thorns did in the return of Gomer to Hosea is very interesting. Hosea 2:7 says:

And she shall follow after her lovers, but she shall not overtake them; and she shall seek them, but shall not find them. Then shall she say, I will go and return to my first husband; for then was it better than now.

When the hedge principle was applied, Gomer was unable to

keep pace with her illegitimate lovers. Isn't it interesting that as soon as the principle took effect, her sin problems began to flee! The sins that had so easily enslaved her and chased her were now being chased by her. What victory! Moreover, not only did they flee from her, they actually hid from her! Hopeless and abandoned, like the Prodigal Son of Luke 16, Gomer finally realizes that she will return to Hosea for "then it was better than now" (verse 7).

No man will ever genuinely repent until he comes to that moment of truth when he fully sees, and perhaps it is for the very first time, the desperation of his present condition as comparable to that which is the fundamental and universal problem that prevails in the life of every unsaved person. The one who is shackled in sin is incapable of "seeing" the gospel that the child of God quite easily "sees," for II Corinthians 4:3-4 says,

But if our gospel be hidden it is hidden to them' that are lost, In whom the god of this world hath blinded the minds of them who believe not, lest the glorious gospel of Christ, who is the image of God, should shine unto them.

To further substantiate that point, please note the following verse in I Corinthians 2: 14:

But the natural man receiveth not the things of the Spirit of God, ' FOR THEY ARE FOOLISHNESS UNTO HIM, NEITHER CAN HE KNOW THEM, BECAUSE THEY ARE SPIRITUALLY DISCERNED. FOUR STEPS OF PRAYER FOR ' THE SALVATION OF A LOST PERSON

Step One: Recognize That The Unsaved Person Is Spiritually Blind.

Having just discussed the verses relative to this first step, let us now bring the problem into sharper focus. You, like Hosea, have a person for whom you greatly care. That dear person has resisted all your attempts at being reached for the Lord Jesus Christ. You have invited well-qualified and sincere soulwinners to speak with him. but to no avail. Perhaps there was even a time that you were able to persuade your friend to join you in the worship services, and you just knew that he would surely be saved that night - but saved he was not.

Out of frustration with that loved one,_ and impatience with the apparent slowness of God's moving, you became harsh in your insistence. That harsh' manner was Just enough to cause an increased defensiveness to develop in the mood of the one you were trying to win. That, in turn, caused you to become more aggressively hostile in your relationship, and that rugged cycle will continue until you reach a stalemate.

What you need to do is accept without question the Biblical truth we have already noted that that person is unable to see and appreciate the value of salvation. Unless his spiritual eyes are opened, you can "burn the pew" from under him, you can argue with him, you can show him gospel films, you can get him cornered with every evangelist who comes to town, and you can fill his pockets with salvation tracts, but he will never be born again until his eyes are opened to the choice that is his to make. But how can that be accomplished?

Hold on to your seat! For some believers, what is about to be said is brand new territory and is difficult to believe at first. In order to pray effectively for a lost loved one, WE MUST BIND SATAN SO THAT OUR LOVED ONE MAY BE LOOSED AND UNBLINDED, THEN HE WILL BE ABLE TO EXERCISE HIS OWN FREE WILL. The quick response from those hearing of this spiritual tactic for the first time most generally is: "But is it really Biblical that a mere human being like me can actually, can literally, bind the devil?" Indeed, it is! Please note the words of our Lord in Matthew 12:29:

Or else how can one enter into a strong man's house, and spoil his goods, except he first BIND THE STRONG MAN? And then he will spoil his house.

There you have it! Your loved one is imprisoned in the house of the strong man (Satan), and in order for that precious soul to be released, Satan must be bound. So, Step One is not only that you understand the blinded position of the lost but the power that can be yours in releasing him to spiritual sight.

Step Two: Confess Every Known Sin In Your Life.

This is extremely important. Before you enter into any spiritual endeavor, it is vital that sin has been dealt with completely in your own life. Particularly is that important when Satan looms on the horizon as your enemy. You will be doomed to a crushing and devastating defeat if you allow the slightest sin to remain unconfessed in your heart. Psalm 66:18 emphatically declares:

If I regard iniquity in my heart the Lord will not hear me.

In the Book of Acts is the sobering account of some foolish young men who attempted to release another from Satan's power when their own hearts were not pure. Any person who presumes to lay hold on the Prince of Darkness should be fully aware of the dangers and seriousness of his mission as he reads Acts 19: 13-16:

Then certain of the vagabond Jews, exorcists, took upon them to call over them who had evil spirits the name of the Lord Jesus, saying, We adjure you by Jesus, whom Paul preacheth. And there were seven sons of one Sceva, a Jew, and chief of the priests, who did so. And the evil spirit answered and said, Jesus I know, and Paul I know, but who are ye? And the man in whom the evil spirit was, leaped on them and OVERCAME THEM, so that they fled out of that house naked and wounded.

A good approach to take in the cleansing of your heart is to take a sheet of paper and write down each sin that the Spirit brings to your mind. Once your list is completed, take each item before the Lord, agreeing with Him about the fact of the sin and never justifying to yourself the reason you committed that sin. Make a clean break with that particular wrongdoing and appropriate to yourself the promise of I John 1:9:

If we confess our sin, he is faithful and just to forgive us our sin and to cleanse us from all unrighteousness.

As soon as you have discarded each sin and can think of no more sins to place on your list, then turn to God and ask Him to do for you in the same manner as that of David in Psalm 19:12-13:

Who can understand his errors? CLEANSE THOU ME FROM MY SECRET FAULTS. Keep back thy servant also from presumptuous sins; let them not have dominion over me. Then shall I be upright, and I shall be innocent from the great transgression.

"Well," you say, "I must surely be through. I have listed all my sins that have come into my mind, I have dealt with each individually, and I have asked God's forgiveness to cover even the secret sins. There just can't be anything left to do!"

Ah, but there is! One cannot be right with God until he is right with his fellow man. No man can be what he should be vertically until he is what he ought to be horizontally. This means that you are now to take your list one more time and pull from it those sins that involve other people. You must make reconciliation! Matthew 5:23-24 says,

Therefore, if thou bring thy gift to the altar, and there rememberest that thy brother hath ought against thee, Leave there thy gift before the altar, and go thy way; first be reconciled to thy brother, and then come and offer thy gift.

Whoever you have wronged must be approached for forgiveness by an in-person visit., telephone call, or letter. Regardless of how much time has passed since the incident occurred, you must attempt reconciliation.

Included in your correcting of personal relationships is your willingness to forgive others as well as to be forgiven by them. It is a clear teaching of the Word of God that our Lord will not forgive the person who has a spirit of unforgiveness. Matthew 6: 15 says:

But if ye forgive not men their trespasses, neither will your father forgive your trespasses.

Step Three: Examine The Scripture To Learn The Mind Of God About Your Lost Loved One's Most Dominant Sin.

Now that you have made your heart pure from sin so that you can have free access to the sway of God's will, it is now time to concentrate _on that person you want saved. By observance of literally hundreds of such cases, it is obvious that Satan uses a particular sin for which that lost person has a decided weakness to blind the poor man and keep him from the Savior. You must determine what that blinding sin is. Begin a prayerful watch of the unsaved person, asking God to reveal that specific sin which has so plagued and obstructed his opportunity
to be saved.

When God reveals to you the sin that has hobbled and thwarted your acquaintances salvation, turn immediately to your concordance. Do a word study by listing the verses that relate to the particular sin with which you are concerned. Read each verse prayerfully, asking God which verses in the Scriptures would be most helpful to memorize for immediate use in the event of a Satanic attack.

Step Four: Ask The Lord To Redirect The Attacks Of Sin Away From Your Unsaved Loved One And To Yourself.

This, as you by now have already seen, is very serious business. In fact, as a believer willingly allows himself to absorb the attacks of sin that have originally been directed toward the life of another, he learns the lesson of substitution in practice as well as in theory. The believer aligns himself very closely with the Lord Jesus Christ who became man's substitute for him at Calvary. Christ allowed Himself to become the sole target for all of Satan's hellish fury and demonic attack. As He became our sin-bearer, we were released to the illumination of the' Spirit, so that by His quickening power, we could rationally use our will in the acceptance of Christ as Lord. In Luke 19:10 are these words: For the Son of man is come to seek and to save that which was lost.

It' is an assuring thought that the very reason for Christ's coming to earth was that a way of salvation could be provided for us. But even as that was His primary mission, so is it ours: In John 20:21, our Lord directs:

. . . as my Father hath sent me, even so, send I you.

Therefore, to fulfill and follow this explicit commandment of Jesus Christ, we must truly intercede for our loved ones by bearing the attack of sin upon their lives. However, you must be very careful in following very closely the requirements of personal preparation as outlined earlier in Steps Two and Three lest you, like the seven sons of Sceva in Acts 19, should be overtaken and defeated by the very sin that has been blinding the unsaved person.

Here is an example. Several years ago, a lovely young lady came to my office inquiring about how she should pray for her lost husband. In the course of our conversation, she shared that her husband had a lust-filled heart which was difficult for her to understand. She had always been a very sweet and virtuous girl.

Nevertheless she followed the battle plan as outlined already in this chapter:

(1) She recognized him as spiritually blinded.

(2) She confessed every known sin.

(3) She studied the Scriptures about the sin of lust.

(4) She asked that that sin would be released from its control over her husband and passed toward her.

(5) She prayed for the hedge of thorns to encircle her husband while she was confronting his enemy.

In a few weeks, this same young lady returned to my office and brought‘ the expected report. After having followed to the letter my suggestions to her, she found herself bombarded with sexual lusts and thoughts in a manner that she would have previously felt were quite inconceivable. However, because she had done her homework, there were no unconfessed sins to weaken her authoritative position with God and she was ready with her memorized verses to nullify the effect of every challenge. As a result, she was beside herself with joy! What about her husband? About three months later, he was saved!

It is very important to remember that not everyone will be saved. That is unfortunate, but true. You will occasionally have the sad experience of "standing in the gap" for another person only to hear him finally say, "I just do not want God." Generally, when that happens, whether or not you actually hear the person say it, you will have a noticeable lessening of the burden you feel for him until Jeremiah 11:14 will become a living reality:

Therefore pray not thou for this people, neither lift up a cry or a prayer for them: for I will not hear them in the time that they cry unto me for their trouble.

What we have seen in this chapter is God's of prayer for the lost. It is not easy. It is not for the faint hearted nor the immature. Yet, immeasurable vitality will be added to your witness life if you follow this simple outline for success Every soul saved is worth the effort, and more.

PRACTICAL APPLICATIONS
for_
How to Pray for An Unsaved Loved One"

1. Identify the person for whom you have concern and list five possible sins of hindrance to his salvation.

(1)

(2)

(3)

(4)

(5)

2. Use your concordance to find at least one verse to counter each of the above sins.

(1)

(2)

(3)

(4)

(5)

3. In one sentence, state your primary reason for wanting him saved.

4.Plan your attack for a period of one month Each number represents a day of that month Find a verse of praise and give its Bible location

(1)Psalm 92:1

(2)

(3)

(4)

(5)

(6)

(7)

(8)

(9)

(10)

(11)

(12)

(13)

(14)

(15)

(16)

(17)

(18)

(19)

(20)

(21)

(22)

(23)

(24)

(25)

(25)

(27)

(28)

(29)

(30)

Chapter Six

HOW TO SEEK BODILY HEALING

Divine healing is certainly a valid Bible doctrine for today's world. In I Corinthians 12:28 is a partial listing of gifts that were left to the church by the Lord Jesus Christ, and the gift of healing is one of them:

And God hath set some in the church: first apostles, second prophets, third teachers; after that miracles, then gifts of healings, helps, governments, diversities of tongues.

Often the suggestion is made that the gift of divine healing is actually manifested in the skilled hands and minds of those who work in the field of modern medical technology. With the sincerest and most profound respect for those involved in the use of medical techniques for the good of all mankind, that suggestion is simply not valid. The gift of healing is a spiritual gift. The only person who can be a recipient of this gift must be one who has been saved and thereby indwelt by the Spirit of the Living God. Even an unsaved man or woman may develop a skill that is usable in the profession of the healing arts, but only a saved person can be granted the spiritual gift of healing.

Since that is true, and we will discuss more fully the ones who are scripturally authorized to use this gift a little later in the chapter, what may be said about the manner in which healing is being widely debated and developed in our day? Entire electronic ministries are built around healing. Literally hundreds of books are being written on the subject. Scarcely a city in the United States, regardless of size, can pass through a single year without It least one traveling evangelist who advertises himself as leading a "Holy Ghost, spirit-led, soul-saving, healing and deliverance service." The mainline denominations, including even the Roman Catholic Church, has felt schisms within their organizational and doctrinal structures over this very question. Is there a balanced view concerning this vital topic?

The Scriptures are not silent in answer to this question. As is true also with the other spiritual gifts, one should be very careful as he applies the Biblical pattern. Yet, if it fits the pattern, it is of God; if it does not fit the pattern, it is not. There are two extremes, therefore, that an observer may take. One is to label all extraordinary healing activity to be of the Lord while the other view is to label it all of Satan. Both views are in error. Remember, it is very important that we always turn to the Scriptures in matters of doctrinal purity for:

All scripture is given by inspiration of God. And IS PROFITABLE FOR DOCTRINE, for reproof. For instruction in righteousness: That the man of Gad may be perfect, thoroughly furnished unto all good works (II Timothy 3:16-17).

It is at this very point of scriptural authority that many sincere people in the "healing movements" make their mistake. We cannot distort the Scriptures to make them say what we want to hear. While there are many applications of a given truth found in a particular passage, there is still only one interpretation of that passage. To make an application without first seeing the interpretation constitutes faulty Bible scholarship. And that is done so frequently in the proof-texts of those most involved in healing ministries.

THE INTERPRETATION or ISAIAH 53:5

Let me share an example. The basic argument of the "health and wealth" preacher is that our physical healing was purchased at Calvary. He argues that if, as everyone agrees, our spiritual healing was purchased at Calvary and is available to all who desire it, even so is physical healing available to all who will look to the cross for its appropriation for the bodily needs of their lives. Used as proof is Isaiah 53:5 which reads:

But he was wounded for our transgressions, he was bruised for our iniquities, the chastisement of our peace was upon him, and with his stripes we are healed.

As you already undoubtedly know, this verse is part of a more extended passage in Isaiah 53 that primarily concerns itself with the crucifixion of our Lord. To accurately understand the message of this verse, it must first be read in the context of adjoining verses. It is poor Bible scholarship indeed that pulls a single phrase from a lengthy passage and builds a major doctrinal position upon it. if that were acceptable, we could pull the phrase in Matthew 27:5 about Judas that says he "went and hanged himself," combine that with another and totally unrelated command in Luke 10:37: "Go, and do thou likewise," and add this phrase in John 13:27: "What thou doest, do quickly." Now we have a great Bible doctrine that exhorts us to quickly go out and hang ourselves! Of course, we would all agree that this very notion is preposterous and yet we apply the same foolish procedures in developing interpretations of more serious scriptural truths.

If we are to understand correctly the message of "with his stripes we are healed" in Isaiah 53:5, we must be unafraid to subject this obscure phrase to t-he light of proper study. First, we turn to the original language for the origin of the word, "healed." The word that is found is, "sozo." "Sozo" may refer to spiritual healing or it may refer to physical healing. To which does it refer; or, is it possible that it can refer to both? Since our word study has not clarified the question, let us move to the second study principle of context.

The writers of the Scriptures always followed patterns of uniformity and consistency. When items were listed and comparisons were made, the writers were always careful to align spiritual with spiritual and physical with physical. Otherwise, throughout the Scriptures would occur a mish-mash and hodge-podge of meanings. Let us now look at the surrounding phrases of "by his stripes we "are healed" and see if we can determine whether this phrase, by contextual meaning, has reference to physical healing or spiritual healing:

But he was wounded for our transgressions, he was bruised for our iniquities; the chastisement of our peace was upon him, and with his stripes we are healed. All we like sheep have gone astray; we have turned every one to his own way, and the Lord hath laid on him the iniquity of us all (Isaiah 53:5-6).

There are three phrases listed before the phrase in question, "by his stripes we are healed," and there are three phrases following it. If we can determine whether these other phrases have references to physical or spiritual conditions, we will then know to which the phrase in question has reference. "But he was wounded for our transgressions" is obviously spiritual, since "transgressions," the key word, is in reference to sin. The same is also true of "he was bruised for our iniquities"; therefore, it too is spiritual. "The chastisement of our peace" is spiritual because inner peace is a spiritual condition. Now we see that the three preceding phrases are, without question or doubt, related to the spiritual.

In verse six are the three phrases that follow the one in question. "All we like sheep have gone astray" is a metaphorical description of mankind in sin and away from God and is, therefore, spiritual. "We have turned everyone to his own way" is a statement of man's sinful nature, so it is also listed as spiritual. "The Lord hath laid on him the iniquity of us all" must be spiritual since the key word is "iniquity" which is another word for sin.

What have we found by contextual analysis? The three phrases prior to our phrase of obscure meaning all refer to spiritual conditions; the three phrases following refer to spiritual conditions. Therefore, consistent with proper scholarship and common sense, "by his stripes we are healed speaks of man's spiritual healing, not his physical healing.

In fact, it was not necessary for Christ to die in order for Him to display his healing power. Isaiah is very careful in his separation of Christ's authority over the physical and the spiritual by separating Isaiah 53:4, which deals with man's physical ails, and Isaiah 53:5-6, which deals with man's spiritual difficulties. He makes that definite separation with the use of the conjunction, "but," as the first word in verse five, to show that he has been speaking of one area (physical) and now he will be looking at an entirely different area (spiritual). Isaiah 53:4 reads:

> *Surely he hath borne our grief, and carried our sorrows; yet we did esteem him stricken, smitten of God, and afflicted.*

For the fulfillment of that verse in the life of Christ, read the following account in Matthew 8: 14-17:

> *And when Jesus was come into Peter's house, he saw his wife's mother laid, and sick of a fever. And he touched her hand, and the fever left her; and she arose, and ministered unto them. When the even was come, they brought unto him many that were possessed with devils; and he cast out the spirits with his word, and healed all that were sick: HE HIMSELF TOOK OUR INFIRMITIES, AND BORE OUR SICKNESSES.*

Would you please note that our physical healing could as easily have been accomplished had we lived prior to Calvary as now? Man's physical healing requires only the Word of Jesus; man's spiritual healing required His death.

But why does man suffer sickness? There are several reasons often given, but it seems that the Scriptures give only three: sin, the devil, and God. Everyone who suffers should first determine the cause, among these three, for his suffering.

SIN MAY CAUSE SUFFERING

First, sin, either directly or indirectly, causes sickness. Every member of the human family will at some time suffer sickness because of the introduction of sin as a result of the fall of Adam. From that point of transgression by the federal head of the human race, man's body has inherited the condition of continual deterioration. More directly, poor habits of diet and bodily abuse and clear acts of sin (i.e. drugs, alcohol, illicit sex)' have resulted in sickness for multitudes of people. Sin can lead to sickness. Paul encourages the believer to use an observance of the Lord's Supper as a time of self-Judgment in I Corinthians 11:27-30:

Wherefore, whosoever shall eat this bread, and drink this cup of the Lord, unworthily, shall be guilty of the body and blood of the Lord. But let a man examine himself, and so let him eat of that bread, and drink of that cup, For he that eateth and drinketh unworthily, eateth and drinketh damnation to himself, not discerning the Lord's body. FOR THIS CAUSE MANY ARE WEAK AND SICKLY AMONG YOU, AND MANY SLEEP.

When a Christian sins, the Holy Spirit indwelling him will disturb him to the urgent need of repentance. If the believer refuses to judge himself and repent, God will begin his chastising work in the believer's life as described in the twelfth chapter of Hebrews. This chastisement may take the form of physical illness, financial adversity, emotional instability, etc. It may even include premature death by which the believer is removed from the world. Note again the last three words of I Corinthians ll:30, ". . . and many sleep," which is a New Testament term for a believer's death. This sin that may result in death is also confirmed in I John 5:16:

If any man see his brother sin a sin which is not unto death, he shall ask, and he shall give him life for them that sin not unto death. THERE IS A SIN UNTO DEATH: I do not say that he shall pray for it.

THE DEVIL MAY CAUSE SUFFERING

Second, not only does sin cause sickness, but the devil causes sickness. There is a precious story found in the thirteenth chapter of Luke. Christ comes to the synagogue on the Sabbath. As He is teaching the people, His eyes fall upon a poor woman who is "bowed together." What a pitiful sight she must have been. Her self-esteem was surely low. Of this poor creature Jesus says after healing her:

And ought not this woman, being a daughter of Abraham, WHOM SATAN HATH BOUND, LO, THESE EIGHTEEN YEARS, be loosed from this bond on the Sabbath day? (Luke 13:16).

And, what of Job? This Old Testament saint was the very epitome of suffering. He suffered mentally at the death of his family, emotionally at the taunts of his wife, socially at the lack of understanding by his friends, spiritually at his questions about God's will for him, financially at the loss of his possessions, and physically at the loss of his health. Why did all of these adversities befall Job? In Job 2:6-7 are these words:

And the Lord said unto Satan, Behold, he is in thine hand; but save his life. So went Satan forth from the presence of the Lord, AND SMOTE JOB WITH SORE

BOILS FROM THE SOLE OF HIS FOOT UNTO THE CROWN.

THE LORD MAY CAUSE SUFFERING

Third, not only do sin and the devil cause sickness, but often our Lord allows sickness so that He may receive more glory for Himself. As God receives more glory, His kingdom is expanded by the souls who are saved. Glory may be defined as "the outward manifestation of an inward reality" and as such is often best exhibited in the patient endurance of sickness by the saints of God. The Apostle Paul is an excellent example:

And lest I should be exalted above measure through the abundance of the revelations, there was given to me a thorn in the flesh, the messenger of Satan to buffet me, lest I should be exalted above measure. For this thing I besought the Lord thrice, that it might depart from me. And he said unto me, my grace is sufficient for thee; for MY STRENGTH IS MADE PERFECT IN WEAKNESS. Most gladly, therefore, will I RATHER GLORY IN MY INFIRMITIES, THAT THE POWER OF CHRIST MAY REST UPON ME. Therefore, I TAKE PLEASURE IN INFIRMITIES, in reproaches, in necessities, in persecutions, in distresses for Christ's sake; FOR WHEN I AM WEAK THEN AM I STRONG (II Corinthians 12-7-10).

We know that Paul was a man of great faith and a man of great spiritual power. He abhorred the very presence of sin in his life. Yet, he suffered sickness. Paul understood something that many in the "healing movements' have failed to learn. Sometimes it is God's will for the saint to suffer. In the above-quoted verges, one can clearly see the spiritual advantages accrued by Paul as a result of

God allowing sickness in his life. By Paul's own testimony we know that he believed the advantages far outweighed the disadvantages.

Another New Testament saint who found joy in Gods service through sickness was Epaphroditus, a companion of Paul in the work-of the Lord. In Philippians 2:25-27 the account of his sickness is given:

Yet I supposed it necessary to send to you Epaphroditus, my brother and companion in labor, and fellow soldier, but your messenger, and he that ministered to my wants. For he longed after you all, and was full of heaviness, because ye had heard that he had been sick. For, indeed, HE WAS SICK NIGH unto DEATH, but God had mercy on him, ' and not on him but on me also, lest I should have sorrow upon sorrow.

Paul was grateful that the Lord chose to spare the life Of Epaphroditus. However, he realized that the serious illness that Epaphroditus had suffered was actually good for the work of God. He says, in Philippians 2:29-30:

Receive him, therefore, in the Lord with all gladness, and hold such in reputation, Because, FOR THE WORK OF CHRIST, HE WAS NIGH UNTO DEATH, NOT REGARDING HIS LIFE, to supply your lack of service toward me.

Another of Paul's friends was a man by the name of Trophimus. Remember, Paul was a devout and Spirit» filled follower of the Lord Jesus Christ. He was also a great man of prayer. It is inconceivable that if every sick person is intended by the Lord to be healed through the power of faith that anyone so blessed as to be loved by Paul could possibly remain sick. That is, however, precisely what happened in the case of Trophimus:

Erastus abode at Corinth; but Trophimus have I left at Miletus sick (II Timothy 4:20).

Sometimes the greatest ministries we will ever see performed are by those who continue to serve the Lord in spite of personal difficulty. Think clearly. If sickness is never in the will of God and is always proof positive of the sufferer's alienation from God, then it would seem logical that the Lord could never use that person until he recovered. The holiness of the Lord would not allow it. An example from the Scriptures that utterly disproves the absurdity of such logic is found in II Kings 13:14 about the prophet, Elisha:

Now Elisha WAS FALLEN SICK WITH HIS SICKNESS OF WHICH HE DIED.

Was Elisha in the will of God while he was terminally ill? The Bible records that he was. Verses fifteen through nineteen of the same chapter shares one of the Bibles most astonishing prophecies, and it came from the lips of Elisha while he was deathly sick. It is obvious, then, that man is not limited in his usefulness to God because of personal disease. Sometimes the disease only serves to accentuate the beauty of God's message THROUGH the one who suffers TO others who are near.

THE PATTERN OF PRAYER FOR HEALING

Recognizing that the Bible does not teach that God has chosen to heal everyone and finding ample verses to affirm God's compassion for the sick, what is to be
the believer's stance? Is there a way to pray for our diseased loved ones? Indeed, there is! In James 5:10-15, the procedure for prayer for the sick is given:

Take, my brethren, the prophets who have spoken in the name of the Lord, for an example of suffering affliction, and of patience. Behold, we count them happy who endure. Ye have heard of the patience of Job, and have seen the end of the Lord, that the Lord is very pitiful and of tender mercy, . . . Is any sick among you? Let him call for the elders of the church; and let them pray over him, anointing him with oil in the name of the Lord; And the prayer of faith shall save the sick, and the Lord shall raise him up; and if he have committed sins, they shall be forgiven him.

Verse ten contains a very important thought: "Take, my brethren, the prophets who have spoken in the name of the Lord, FOR AN EXAMPLE OF SUFFERING AFFLICTION, AND OF PATIENCE." Again, James quickly asserts that some of God's choicest servants have with gladness suffered patiently according to the perfect will of the Lord.

Nevertheless, in the fourteenth verse of the chapter, James begins his description of the means by which a person may approach the Lord on behalf of one who is ill. You must remember that the church is "the body of Christ" (I Corinthians 12:27) in the world today. The demonstration of God's power was manifested in and through Christ's physical body when He walked upon the earth. Even so, the authority and power of God has been manifested in and through the church, which is His body, ever since His bodily resurrection and ascension. As well-meaning as extra-church activities (i.e. gospel fellowships, home Bible studies, stadium faith meetings, healing services) may be, the power of God is reserved for the guardianship and authority of the church. Be wary of any individual or organization that is either anti-church or presumes itself to lend power to the church. For whatever faults the church may possess, "Christ also loved the church, and gave himself for it" (Ephesians 5:25).

It is little wonder, then, that James exhorts the sick, in verse fourteen, to call for the elders of the church. The word, "elders," may be translated "bishops" or "pastors." We may be quite comfortable and correct in applying the term to the leadership of the local church. For us to enjoy the blessings that our Lord has reserved for us, we must always follow the Biblical pattern. The pattern is not for a faith healer to set up a service in a tent or coliseum and ask the sick to come to him. That is opposite the command that is found in verse fourteen where we are taught that the sick are to call for the leaders of the church to come to them.

After the elders arrive, the Scriptures say they are to "pray over him." Closely connected to that prayer is the next statement which adjures them to "anoint him with oil in the name of the Lord." Many have suggested that that anointing has reference to medical treatment. However, quite honestly, the anointing of oil followed the example and meaning of the anointing of oil in the Old Testament as the priests used it to sanctify and set apart temple vessels for worship. It seems quite clear that James is suggesting that THE

ELDERS SHOULD PRAY FOR A KNOWLEDGE OF GOD'S WILL CONCERNING THE SICK ONE'S RECOVERY WHILE THEY PRESENT HIM AS A SANCTIFIED VESSEL for use to God's glory. As they prayerfully ascertain God's will in the matter, they claim it as done and are able, as a result, to have the assurance that "the prayer of faith shall save the sick, and the Lord shall raise him up (verse 15).

How often it occurs that many handicapped and seriously ill believers are led by faith healers to believe that the reason for their continued illness is their own lack of faith. Please note that it is not the faith of the sick person that results in healing. It is the faith of the one who is praying for him. When failure occurs in the faith healer's ministry, as is so often the case, he would be more respected would he admit, according to James 5:15, that HIS faith, not that of the sick, was faulty.

What should we do when sick? As we initiate our use of the most advanced medical techniques available, we ought to call upon those who lead the church where we worship. We are then to present ourselves as instruments fit for God's service, determined that regardless of the outcome of our state of health, we will glorify Him! Though like those of the world, we must suffer; we must not suffer like the world! Whether He chooses to heal us miraculously, whether we are made well by medicine, or whether we remain sick, the condition of our body will never adversely affect the condition of our spirit. We are the Lord's.

PRACTICAL APPLICATIONS
for
"How to Seek for Bodily Healing"

1. Write a brief description of your philosophy of life.

2. Use your concordance to do a word study on heal, healed, and healing. Write each reference below and prayerfully study them for meaning.

3. Write one sentence telling what you believe about divine healing.

4. Write the name of one physically ill person. Before praying for his or her healing, pray for God to reveal to you His ultimate will in the

case of that person. Pray for that revelation until you sense God has given it,

5. Imagine that you are seriously ill. Based on what you have read in this chapter, what will you do?

Chapter Seven

HOW TO LIVE IN THE POWER OF THE SPIRIT

Many years ago, there was a meeting of religious leaders in a particular city. They were brought together as a result of their mutual desire to see a spiritual awakening occur in their area. After considerable deliberation, it was determined that an evangelist should be invited to lead a series of revival crusade meetings of several weeks' duration. But who would that evangelist be? Several names were suggested, but the name of Dwight L. Moody continued to recur as they prayerfully sought God's will. in exasperation, one of the participants blurted, "Moody! All l hear is Moody! Does Moody have more of God than anyone else?" To that emotional query came the quietly profound answer by another, "No, Dwight L. Moody does not have more of God than anyone else, but God has more of Dwight L. Moody!"

HOLY GHOST BAPTISM

One of the most amazing Bible facts is that every believer has just as much of God's presence in his life as does any other, including any great Christian leader who may be named. Every believer has as much of God as did Peter, James, Paul, Martin Luther, Charles Spurgeon,
Dwight Moody, Charles Finney, Billy Sunday or Campbell Morgan. He has as much of God available to him as Billy Graham, W. A. Criswell, Charles Stanley, or James Kennedy. The moment a person

is saved, God indwells him:

> *But ye are not in the flesh, but in the Spirit, if so be that the Spirit of God indwell you. NOW IF ANY MAN HAVE NOT THE SPIRIT OF CHRIST, HE IS NONE OF HIS (Romans 8:9).*

There it is! One must come to the place of knowing, really knowing, that the Spirit of Power does not come at some point AFTER salvation as many suggest. That is an absolute impossibility as the above verse clearly states! It is by the precious baptism provided by the Holy Ghost that we enter into union with Christ and our fellow believers:

> *For as the body is one, and hath many members, and all the members of that one body, being many, are one body: so also is Christ. For by one Spirit, are we all baptized into one body, whether we be bond or free; and have been all made to drink into one Spirit (I Corinthians 12:11-13).*

This baptism, which takes place at salvation, provides the Holy Ghost a place to RESIDE. He comes into the believer's life and will never leave it:

> *And I will pray the Father, and He shall give you another Comforter, that HE MAY ABIDE WITH YOU FOREVER, even the Spirit of truth; whom the world cannot receive, because it seeth him not, neither knoweth him; but ye know him; FOR HE DWELLETH WITH YOU, AND SHALL BE IN YOU (Romans 14:16-17).*

Your life, as a believer, has become the temple of God:

What? Know ye not that your body is the temple of the Holy Ghost which is in you, which ye have of God, and ye are not your own? For ye are bought with a price; therefore, glorify God in your body, and in your spirit, which are God's (I Corinthians 6:19-20).

Since the promise is ours that the Holy Spirit views the believer's body as His own personal temple and that He gives the assurance of never leaving, it now becomes quite clear why the believer experiences such anguish and turmoil when he sins. The holiness of God that lives within him will not permit the unholiness of the world to enter. Sin and the Spirit cannot, and will not, co-exist. They are alien and opposite to each other.

But remember, the baptism of the Spirit is the means by which God indwells the believer, never to depart even when there is the introduction of sin, and He enters the believer's life at the time of that person's salvation. He RESIDES in every Christian's life.

HOLY GHOST FILLING

Unfortunately, however, the Spirit is not allowed to PRESIDE in the life of each believer, and that sad plight is due to the apathy and sorry state of sin into which most Christians have fallen. Although there is only one baptism, there are many fillings of the Spirit, and that is the process by which the Spirit presides. Peter, the flaming evangelist on the day of Pentecost, for example, was himself filled with the dominating control of the Spirit at various times in the Book of Acts:

And they were all FILLED WITH THE HOLY GHOST. . . . But Peter, standing up with the eleven, lifted up his voice, and said unto them, Ye men of Jerusalem, be this known unto you, and hearken to my words (Acts 2:4, 14).

Then Peter, FILLED WITH THE HOLY GHOST, said unto them . . . (Acts 4:8).

But Peter and John answered and said unto them, Whether it be right in the sight of God to hearken unto you more than unto God, judge ye . . . And when they had prayed, the place was shaken where they were assembled together; and THEY WERE ALL FILLED WITH THE HOLY GHOST, and they spake the Word of God with boldness (Acts 4:19, 31).

By and large, the church of today views the filling of the spirit with either fearful skepticism or an attitude of "take-it-or-leave-it." This precious doctrine has been so frequently misunderstood that it has now been relegated to the frenetic emotionalism of those more deeply involved in Pentecostalism and almost excluded from practical application in the organizational life and decision-making of the main-line denominations. However, the filling of the Spirit is to be neither feared nor ignored. Actually, every believer is commanded to be filled.

And be not drunk with wine, wherein is excess; but BE FILLED WITH THE SPIRIT (Ephesians 5:18).

This verse contains a direct commandment from the Lord, and to disobey any of His commands is sin. We are not asked to be filled, suggested to be filled, or pleaded by the Lord to be filled. WE ARE COMMANDED BY HIM TO BE FILLED WITH HIS SPIRIT!

It is indeed paradoxical that we will accept so readily one part of a Bible statement and perform it faithfully and will just as quickly refuse compliance with another part. Any church would be horrified to see its pastor intoxicated on a Sunday morning; yet, the majority of even evangelical churches take little note as whether the pastor is filled with the Spirit as he steps into the pulpit. According to Ephesians 5:18, however, every believer is just as emphatically commanded to be filled as he is to abstain from drunkenness. Therefore, a person may be morally upright in every respect, but if he fails to be filled he has sinned as much as the man who is morally bankrupt. Unless you understand the serious implications of that failure, you will never have the power outwardly manifested that inwardly resides.

THE FILLING AND COMPLETE AUTHORITY

It is critical that you understand what the filling with the Spirit means. Quite often, sincere Bible teachers try to explain the Spirit's filling by using the old illustration of pouring water into a gallon bucket. When the bucket has been filled to the brim and there is nothing else in it but water, the parallel with the filling of the Spirit in the believer is complete. That sounds good, but it is just not an accurate portrayal.

A better analogy is a man and his house. He has a key to every room, drawer, closet, and cabinet. There is nothing that is locked to him. The house is yielded to his control and authority. So it should also be in the life of every person who knows God. The sweet Holy Spirit ought to be welcome in every phase of the individual's life with no area declared off-limits. When that glad condition exists, the believer can honestly say that he is filled with the Spirit.

But now we have arrived at a very controversial and generally misunderstood point. Assuming that one has fully accepted what has been previously pointed out in this chapter concerning the baptism of the Spirit and the multiple fillings with the Spirit, how does the believer make that filling a practical, day-by-day reality in his life? Volumes have been written, long sermon series have been preached, and seminars have been conducted that have all attempted to address themselves to this serious proposition.

It may seem simplistic and trite, but Southern Baptist evangelist, Sam Cathey, made an interesting and accurate observation at the 1982 Florida Baptist Convention Evangelism Conference in Tallahassee when he responded to the question of the Spirit's filling by saying in his own inimitable manner, "Quit sinning!" Really, he is right! Sin is the only obstruction to the free flow of the Spirit into any area of the Christian's life. If the sins are eliminated by honest introspection, confession, and personal self-judgment, the believer is then utterly filled and controlled by the Spirit of God.

HOLY SPIRIT LIVING

Closely connected with the issue of sin is the willingness by the Spirit-filled believer to make God's desires his primary motivation and first priority. In virtually every Old Testament and New Testament account of great individual deeds being performed, the one who displayed the authority of God in the performance of those deeds always operated by a very important Bible principle. That principle, so necessary in the exercise of Spirit power, is the conscious effort to consider always the wishes of God before any other considerations — including one's own personal desires. We will examine a few of the more out-standing examples in the Word 'of God. An excellent illustration is found in Joshua 3: 13 where the children of Israel are attempting to cross the Jordan River:

> *And it shall come to pass, AS SOON AS THE SOLES OF THE FEET OF THE PRIESTS THAT BEAR THE ARK OF THE LORD, the Lord of all the earth, shall rest in the waters of Jordan, that the waters of Jordan shall be CUT OFF FROM THE WATERS that come down from above; and they shall stand upon an heap.*

What is it that God has tried to show his people about power from the very beginning? He has been putting man into "impossible" situations where failure and frustration are certain without His intervention. It is not that God has some mysterious need to know man's limitations, be- cause, being sovereign, He already knows. What He does achieve by placing man into "no-win" predicaments is the satisfaction of fellowship with the man who finally sees his own frailty when contrasted with the Lord's infinite power. Perhaps you can more easily understand the message in I Corinthians 1:26-29:

> For ye see your calling, brethren, how that NOT MANY WISE men after the flesh, NOT MANY MIGHTY, NOT MANY NOBLE, are called: But God hath chosen the foolish things of the world to con- found the wise; and God hath chosen the weak things 0/ the world to confound the things which are mighty; and base things of the world, and things which are despised, hath God chosen, yea, and things which are not, to bring to nought things that are: THAT NO FLESH SHOULD GLORY IN HIS PRESENCE.

But what, pray tell, do the foregoing observations have to do with the children of Israel at Jordan? Very simply God was showing in this narrative at Jordan, as He does in so many other incidents throughout the Scriptures, that the commandments of God may not appear reasonable to the logic of man, but nevertheless they can be implicitly trusted. In the process, the Israelites learned that God was expecting them to expend all of their abilities and powers after which He would share His own power with them. This whole scenario brought the application of "no flesh should glory in His presence" very vividly into the fabric of Israel's national consciousness.

Try to imagine what may have taken place as the Israelites formerlystood in long lines along the banks of the Jordan River. Two questions continued to be asked by just about everyone. Why did God choose this season of the year for the crossing when there were other times in the year during which the water level was much lower? Secondly, how in the world would they ever get across? Dejected because of the inability of their experts to arrive at a satisfactory answer, the multitudes waited in hopeless despair for an answer from God.

And what an answer He gave, but it certainly surprise them! Man has always had a tendency to look backward from a difficulty toward previous similar problem through which he has already passed. In the hope that he will find a key to unlocking God s ways for the present dilemma. Without doubt, the host of Israelites recalled what their parents had told them about the crossing of the Red Sea. But the veteran leader, Moses. had been present there, and now they were being led by the novice and unproven Joshua. What would God do? The consensus opinion was that the Lord would probably do as He had done at the Red Sea by rolling the water back and leaving a dry path for them to walk upon.

How surprised they must have been when the word came to them that God would indeed roll the water back AFTER the priests' feet had been placed in the Jordan. Most believers in the modem church have difficulty in accepting that approach, too.

Man says, "I will tithe when I have the money."

God says, "If you will tithe, I will see that you have the money."

Man says, "I will teach a Sunday School class when I learn the Bible a little better."

God says, "If you will teach the class, you will learn the Bible better."

Man says, "I will go witnessing during our church visitation program when I learn the proper soul winning techniques."

God says, "If you will go witnessing, you will develop better skills and techniques in soul winning." '

This is a vital principle for the Spirit-filled Christian. GOD WILL NEVER SHARE HIS AWESOME POWER WITH THE BELIEVER UNTIL THAT BELIEVER HAS USED THE POWER THAT HE ALREADY POSSESSES.

By waiting until all mortal strength is gone and human planning has failed, God places the believer in a position of never questioning the source of the victory. With assurance, the Christian can move forward in his spiritual growth with more confidence in the providential care of the Father for His children.

If this were the only incident depicting this important principle, it would be sufficient; but there are others that corroborate this basic expectation of God for man's proper ordering of priorities. No man is filled with the Spirit who does not practice a lifestyle guided by this principle.

GIDEON

We can see this same lesson applied in the life of Gideon who is generally remembered for his courageous trust in the leadership of God. It is not often remembered that he had his moments of cowardice. Note carefully where Gideon was found by the angel when he was threshing wheat.

And there came an angel of the Lord, and sat under an oak which was in Ophrah, that pertained unto Joash the Abiezrite: and his son Gideon THRESHED WHEAT BY THE WINEPRESS, TO HIDE IT FROM THE MIDIANITES (Judges 6:11).

Gideon was threshing wheat at the winepress. That is significant! Areas for threshing wheat were located on the tops of hills so that as the wheat was thrown into the air the breeze would separate the wheat and the chaff. Wine-presses were located in small valleys or gulleys. To accomplish the threshing of wheat near a winepress was made more difficult because of the lack of free flowing breezes, but so it always is when a follower of God fails to take open steps of faith in his work for the Lord. Whatever is done for Him under such circumstances of fear are less than glorious and always hard.

It would have been unbelievably sad if Gideon had stayed in hiding from the Midianitess Israel could not have been delivered from its enemy, Gideon's. name would have been blemished beyond repair, and all of us who live by faith would have been robbed of one of our greatest faith heroes. But can't we be glad that God knows us better than we know ourselves. Gideon considered himself a coward; God saw Gideon as a "man of valor." Note the following verses from Judges 6: 12-I3:

And the angel of the Lord appeared unto him, and said unto him, The Lord is with thee, THOU MIGHTY MAN OF VALOR. And Gideon said unto him, Oh my Lord, if the Lord be with us, why then is all this befallen us? And where be all his miracles which our fathers told us of, saying, Did not the Lord bring us up from Egypt? But now the Lord hath forsaken us, and delivered us into the hands of the Midiamtes.

It is interesting that the outward circumstances certainly did not give evidence of valor in the heart of Gideon. If he was waiting for some spectacular miracle sign from God, as many would-be warriors in this. present age do, he was destined for frustration. God did not have a miracle for him, at least not yet, but He did have some important advice:

And the Lord looked upon him and said, GO IN THIS THY MIGHT, and thou shalt save Israel from the hands of the Midianites:

Have not I sent thee? (Judges 6:14).

God's word to Gideon was, "Gideon, you take WHAT you have and ALL you have and enter directly into the conflict. When you come to the outer limits of your own strength and you have exhausted all your resources, I will then come to your side with all the power of heaven. How could Gideon possibly lose? His only weakness was the weakness of limited vision, but even vision is enlarged when looking through the eyes of God.

THE WIDOW OF ZAREPHATH

Our next example of great Bible characters who first used the power they already possessed in making God's glory their primary concern is found in I Kings 17. In order to position the account with which we will deal, it should be remembered that Elijah had been led of the
Lord to the brook called Cherith. He was brought to the brook because there was a drought in the land and God desired him in a definite place to be fed by the ravens. But remember, though God may lead a person to a particular place of service, this incident in the life of Elijah affirms that God may choose to move a God-directed person from a God-directed place to yet another place.

So, Elijah makes another trek. This time, he leaves the rural pastoral tranquility of an isolated life to the teeming hustle-and-bustle of urban living. He goes to the city of Zarephath. Upon his arrival there, Elijah finds the woman to whom he had been directed. The story is a very familiar one, but it is such a very important one in relation to the subject at hand. Let us look at it again, paying particular attention to the words that are highlighted for emphasis.

And the word of the Lord came unto him, saying, Arise, get thee to Zarephath, which belongeth to Zidon, and dwell there: behold, I HAVE COMMANDED A WIDOW WOMAN TO SUSTAIN THEE. So he arose and went to Zarephath. And when he came to the gate of the city, behold, the widow woman was there gathering sticks: and he called to her, and said, fetch me, I pray thee, a little water in a vessel, that I may drink. And as she was going to fetch it, he called to her, and said, Bring me, I pray thee, a morsel of bread in thine hand. And she said, As the Lord thy God liveth, I have not a cake, but an handful of meal in a barrel, and a little oil in a cruse: and behold, I am gathering two that I may go in and dress it for me and my son, that we may eat it, and die. And Elijah said unto her, Fear not; GO AND DO AS THOU HAST SAID: but MAKE ME THEREOF, A LITTLE CAKE FIRST, and bring it unto me, and after make for thee and for thy son. For thus saith the Lord God of Israel, the barrel of meal shall not waste, neither shall the cruse of oil fail, until the dat that the Lord sendeth rain upon the earth. And SHE WENT AND DID ACCORDING TO THE SAYING of Elijah and she and he and her house, did eat many days. AND THE BARREL OF MEAL WASTED NOT, NEITHER DID THE CRUSE OF OIL FAIL, ACCORDING TO THE WORD OF THE LORD, which he spake by Elijah (1 Kings 17:8-16).

Often, faithful Bible preachers are urged by well meaning but misdirected church members to be more careful as they preach on tithing in order that the very poor people will not be hurt or embarrassed. The nominal Christian seems to feel that only financially secure people should hear sermons on material stewardship. The exact opposite is true. If there is anyone who needs to hear about God's plain expectations, it is the poor unfortunate should who is barely "making ends meet. He needs to be taught that just like the poor widow with two mites encountered by Jesus, there is something that can be given and God expects him to give it. Please note that in the case of Elijah in Kings 17:9 she was under a direct command of God to feed God's man. In other words, she was to do what she could with what she had and, in the process, make God's services her first priority. Read the following in I Kings 17:9:

Arise, get thee to Zarephath, which belongeth to Zidon, and dwell there, BEHOLD, I HAVE COMMANDED A WIDOW WOMAN TO SUSTAIN THEE.

Had Elijah failed in pressing the woman to follow God's commandment because of his compassion for her adverse circumstances, he would have caused her to miss the beautiful blessings that God had reserved for her. On the other hand, this woman had at least two apparently valid reasons for not complying with the request of Elijah. She could have insisted, as many carnal believers do in the church of today, that "charity begins at home." After all she had been given the responsibility of caring for a child. What about him?

Second, she might have excused herself by saying that it was no concern for her that this stranger needed food, because everyone needed food as a result of the famine in the land. This reason, couched in the modern vernacular, would be framed in the excuse that the church does not need money as much as the family. Yet, just as Elijah represented God's power in Israel at this point in history, even so does the church represent God's power in the world of the twentieth century. Every Christian should be made aware that however hard it may seem, God's representative — be it Elijah or be it the church — is to receive first priority support or else God will not provide for the individual's own needs.

But this poor widow moved quickly to do as Elijah had directed. In one of the more humorous by-lines in the Scriptures, as she returned again and again to the barrel of meal, the original handful continued to replace itself. Without doubt this was the beginning of "self-rising meal." Her needs were met, her son's needs were met, Elijah's needs were met, and all of these needs were supplied because this faithful little widow took the little that she possessed and gave it to God. Again, as with the Israelites at Jordan, this incident shows quite clearly that
God extends His great power to man when man extends his feeble power to God.

For a Christian to do as this poor widow did and receive the necessary supply from God sufficient to the meeting of whatever needs he is experiencing, there are five things he must see in relation to his particular problem, even as she saw in relation to hers.

First, SHE SAW HER NEED:

Arid she said, As the Lord thy God liveth, I have not a cake, but a handful of meal in a barrel, and a little oil in a cruse; and, behold, I am gathering two sticks that I may go in and dress it for me and my son, that we may eat it, and die (I Kings 17:12).

Optimism is good, but there is an over abundance Of the power of positive thinking existent in the modern pulpit. If we will be honest. with ourselves, there are times that inevitably come to most people. Whether saved or unsaved, that are so heart-wrenching for the individual, that he finds himself unable to think rationally at all, much less positively. In these days of the "how-to manuals" and "inner energy movements" there is a great emphasis on being "number one" by virtue 'of perserverance and pride. We must nevertheless be painfully aware that without God we are terribly destitute and deeply in need. Unless we see that need of Him, we will never appropriate to ourselves the power that is available to us.

Second, SHE SAW WHAT SHE NEEDED TO DO:

And Elijah said unto her, Fear not; go and do as thou hast said: but MAKE ME THEREOF A LITTLE CAKE FIRST, and bring it unto me, and after make for thee and for thy son (I Kings 17:13).

Whenever God has something for a man to do, He is always specific. Just as this poor woman was told in precise terms the exact plan that God had for her and she did it, the believer must respond in agreeable acquiescence to God's directives and will. The truly spiritual man does not get so caught up with the "great" aspects of his religious service that he fails to perform the little requirements. Many young preachers are willing to fill in for Billy Graham at one of his crusades, but find it "out of God's will" to do supply preaching at a mission church where no more than fifteen people will be present. One young lady in San Francisco felt the definite call of God on her life to go to China as a missionary, but she could not bring herself to witness in the Chinatown part of the city in conjunction with her church's visitation program. The Spirit-filled man is more concerned about God's reputation than his own, and he is willing to do whatever is best to enhance the name of God in the minds of the world. No task is too big; no job is too little.

Third, SHE SAW THAT HER GREATER NEED WAS TO BELIEVE THE WORD OF GOD:

For thus saith the Lord God of Israel, The barrel of meal shall not waste, neither shall the cruse of oil fail, until the day that the Lord sendeth rain upon the earth (I KingsI7:14).

God made her an almost unbelievable promise. But remember, she had nothing to lose. Her original plan was to make cakes for herself and her son; and then die. As illogical as God's promises may sound, what more can the world offer? Despair and loss are the twin wages of of the man of the world. Death is the calling card of the devil. The only people with even a modicum of happiness and security are those who live by the trustworthiness of the Word of God.

This is the age of computer science and intelligent reason. Secular humanism has seen to that. It is not the age of faith without confirmation. This paralyzing philosophy has been infiltrating and deadening the church with ever-increasing speed. Yet, the Bible message is the same. If a person is to enjoy the demonstration of God's wonder-working power, he must learn the art of believing the Word of God whether his human judgment agrees with that belief or not. In today's church, which has been heavily influenced by the entertainment and promotional- ism of the secular world, our people are asking more and more for some special sign. Whether that sign takes the form of a miraculous healing, an unusual dream, a bequest of an unexpected and large monetary gift, or some unexplained occurrence of an unusual nature, the contemporary believer looks for an affirmation of his faith. He just cannot accept God's Word without visible support.

Many reasons may be offered for the relatively few Spirit-filled men and women that we will meet in our lifetimes, but this has to be one of them. The spiritual man will accept God's Word as the final statement of authority —— period. If there are attending signs —— fine; if not — that is also fine. He lives by the Word. In John 4:46-54 is an account of a man, like the poor widow of I Kings 17, who simply accepted God's Word in a time of dire need. His acceptance of the words of Christ was unattended by signs to support their validity.

Jesus saith unto him, Go thy way; thy son liveth. AND THE MAN BELIEVED THE WORD that Jesus had spoken unto him, and he went his way. And as he was now going down, his servants met him, and told him, saying, Thy son liveth. Then inquired he of them the hour when he began to amend. And they said unto him, YESTERDAY AT THE SEVENTH HOUR THE FEVER LEFT HIM. (John 4:50-51).

What an extraordinary faith! This nobleman did not immediately return to his home after his meeting with Jesus. Had there been the slightest doubt in his mind about the welfare of his son, he could not have gotten home quickly enough! But "he believed the word" so much that he spent the night where he was! That faith in the Word is the quality of faith that God loves to honor This same truth is conveyed by Jesus in John 20:29

Jesus saith unto him, Thomas, because thou hast seen me, thou hast believed: BLESSED ARE THEY THAT HAVE NOT SEEN,

AND YET HAVE BELIEVED.

Fourth, SHE MADE SERVICE T0 GOD HER HIGHEST PRIORITY. In I Kings 17: 15 are these words:

And SHE WENT AND DID ACCORDING TO THE SAYING OF ELIJAH: and she, and he, and her house, did eat many days.

Elijah had instructed her to prepare his meal before she prepared food for herself and her son, and she did exactly what he said. Christianity has its own brand of activism. Ours is not a passive religion that relies on periodic moments of quiet meditation with no challenge to the worshipper for personal testing. Christianity, unlike any other of the world's religions, is built around the person of its founder who is Himself a man of action. And what is His battlecry? "Follow me!" The Spirit-filled man may appear to others in the role of a religious trail-
blazer, but his is not a life of leadership as much as followship.

Fifth, SHE FINALLY POSSESSED HER BLESSING. Growth of any kind is almost always gradual, but the spiritual man patiently waits for the timing of the Lord. Note the realization of her blessing in I Kings 17:16:

And the barrel of meal wasted not, neither did the cruse of oil fail, according to the word of the Lord, which he spake by Elijah.

When the previous four prerequisites are faithfully developed and performed by the believer, he can rest in absolute assurance that the fifth, his needed blessing, will eventually be enjoyed. How long will it be before the church will find its greatest glory by exercising an active faith as this woman did? How long will individual believers be satisfied with a nominal lifestyle devoid of any real blessings? The lesson must be learned! As with Israel at Jordan and Gideon against the Midianites, this woman used what she had, put God's service first, and received the blessings of her Lord in return.

Although there are many other narratives similar to the one just discussed that could be shared in support of the theme we have been developing, suffice it to say that no person will have God's power unless he receives it God's way. Outwardly, the individual may talk the language and appear to be the very epitome of what our Lord expects in the lives of His children and yet be powerless. We really need to learn in these critical days of non-stop "churchianity" that it is far more important what we are than it is what we do. In fact, it is increasingly more evident in the average church that if Satan cannot make a person, or church, bad, he will make them busy.

By any measure, that kind of person will be apathetic in the discharge of genuine Christian service. One has only to speak with the average churchmember of the average church to discover an almost listless attitude about the deeper things of God. A sad portrayal of that condition is found in one of our Lord's letters to one of the seven churches of Asia. In Revelation 3:14-17 are these descriptive words to the church at Laodicea:

And unto the angel of the church of the Laodiceans write: These things saith the Amen, the faithful and true witness, the beginning of the creation of God; I know thy works, that thou art neither cold nor hot, so then because THOU ART LUKEWARM, AND NEITHER COLD NOR HOT, I will spew thee out of my mouth. BECAUSE THOU SAYEST I AM RICH.

AND INCREASED WITH GOODS, AND HAVE NEED OF NOTHING: and knowest not that thou art wretched, and miserable, and poor, and blind, and naked.

This actual historical church is representative of the final segment of the church age just prior to the return of Jesus. Ours is a period in ecclesiastical history that is marked by a callousness to the awfulness of sin, an undue concern for how the church appears to the world rather than how she is viewed by God, and an almost total lack of genuine spiritual power. It is this very kind of church that is seen in the letter to the Laodiceans, but she did not have to resign herself to remaining lukewarm. There was, as there always is for any spiritual predicament, a way of escape provided.

That route of escape was dependent on the principle discussed at considerable length in this chapter — the principle of using whatever power is already available and making God's service a first priority. The verse that confirms this truth is usually used in evangelistic efforts and directed toward lost people. However, the strange twist so pathetically true is that the verse is directed toward saved people in a church where Christ is presumably the head; but sadly, He is outside the door asking for entrance. Please consider the implication of the power principle in Revelation 3:20:

Behold, I stand at the door, and knock: if any man hear my voice, and open the door, I will come in to him, AND WILL SUP WITH HIM AND HE WITH ME.

Obviously, the church at Laodicea had influence, but what the world really needs is not a church of influence, but a church of power. The church had wealth, but the world does not need more wealth, it needs a taste of God's power. Cultured choirs, scholarly pastors, architecturally perfect worship centers, well-oiled programs, and interesting activities have their place, but the one aspect of the church that cannot be made, molded, mooded, or manufactured is the power of God. And the saddest of commentaries is that most churches and individual Christians could continue doing what they are doing without ever once naming the name of Jesus and would suffer no erosion at all in the effectiveness of whatever "ministry" they are performing.

The verse just quoted finds the Lord once more pleading for his followers to use their available resources of power. The phrase, ". . . and will sup with him . . ." very simply means that whatever the church is using for a source of sustenance should be consumed for, by, and with God so that His own divine power might replenish them. Again, as with Israel at Jordan, Gideon with the Midianites, and the widow with Elijah, this church was being challenged to use its own available resources after which God would bring His great power to the forefront in their desperate situation.

Jesus was thinking of this very principle when He said in Matthew 6:33:

But seek ye first the kingdom of God, and his righteousness; and all things shall be added unto you.

The kingdom of God is that entire sphere of our Lord's influence where all beings voluntarily choose to serve him. In this age, it can only be entered by the new birth. Therever every person who would enjoy the blessings of God's provision must first be saved and thereby infused with His Spirit.

A very interesting phrase in this verse is ". . . and his righteousness." Quite clearly, the knowledge of God in a very personal and intimate relationship is of infinitely greater value than only KNOWING ABOUT Him. This explains why theologians sometimes turn into atheists. They know ABOUT God, but they do not know God. Had they ever really known Him personally, they may have developed a dislike for Him because of a variety of reasons, but they could never again doubt His existence.

We began this chapter by relating the story that contained a question about Dwight L. Moody: "Moody! All I hear is Moody. Does Moody have more of God than anyone else?" After reading this chapter, perhaps you can better understand how to obtain the fullness of the power of the Spirit as Moody did. No person is exempted if he has been born of God. It is everyone's privilege. By the application of the three statements of practical Biblical truth discussed in this chapter to the individual life, mundane daily living can be transferred into an adventurous walk with Him! Always remember these three statements:

(1) Holy Spirit baptism takes place at the time of salvation which provides an everlasting residence for Him in the life of the believer;

(2) Holy Spirit filling brings His presiding power as But seek ye first the kingdom of God, and his right- , the believer utterly renounces sin in his life and eousness; and all these things shall be added unto you and gives obedience to God;

(3) Holy Spirit living comes as the believer uses what limited power is at his disposal, places obedience The kingdom of God is. that

entire sphere of our Lord's to God at the top of his priorities and believes the word.

PRACTICAL APPLICATIONS
for
"How to Live in the Power of the Spirit"

1. Identify a very real and specific need in your life. Enter the date of your fasting and prayer for the meeting of that need. Enter the date of the answer.

Need:

Date of Prayer:

Date of Answer:

2. Keep a log of activities for one week. Divide each day into hours. List your major activity during each hour. Example: 7:00-8:00 a.m. — Breakfast. Write a paragraph describing your conclusions after one week.

3. Read a biography on the life of these great Christians and write one sentence about each that describes what you feel were their greatest strengths.

Hudson Taylor

Dwight L. Moody

Corrie Ten Boom

Adoniram Judson

"Praying" Hyde

4. Read each of these books. Write one sentence describing the best lesson you learned from each book.

Life On Its Highest Plane by Ruth Paxson

With Christ In The School of Prayer by Andrew Murray

The Normal Christian Life by Watchman Nee

The Key To Triumphant Living by Jack Taylor

www.ingramcontent.com/pod-product-compliance
Lightning Source LLC
Chambersburg PA
CBHW071952100426
42736CB00043B/2970